Discipline and Discharge
Under the Labor Agreement

Discipline and Discharge Under the Labor Agreement

Walter E. Baer

 AMERICAN MANAGEMENT ASSOCIATION

International standard book number: 0-8144-5296-5
Library of Congress catalog card number: 77-188842
First printing

To Penny, Kris, and Bonnie

Preface

Although parties to labor agreements have achieved and today enjoy a higher level of sophistication than they have had at any time in the past 25 years, discharge and discipline are still too frequently at issue in arbitration cases. An analysis of the many hundreds of published cases on these subjects leads one to conclude that the participants still have a long way to go before they achieve a satisfactory understanding of the rights and responsibilities of each.

There are various reasons for this continuing lack of awareness. Perhaps in part it reflects a failure of all parties—management, labor organizations, and employees—to train themselves and each other as to the proper role of each. Perhaps it also reflects a failure to realize that each is here to stay—that each is entitled to its positions and principles and philosophies—and that the only road to a peaceful and constructive relationship is mutual acceptance, regard, and understanding. But laying this aside and examining only the way most arbitrators view such disputes, we find that they generally concur in their views regarding the bounds of authority of managers and the degree of behavioral freedom of rank-and-file employees.

A management sensitive to the criteria set forth in this book and giving full consideration to all the factors that may influence the outcome of a case should find itself better equipped to defend its action and have it sustained or supported by the arbitrator.

But the final key to resolving such problems is the recognition by each party of the rights of the other. If the number of discipline and discharge cases is ever to be reduced to a more acceptable level, each must assume its educational responsibilities and jointly create an industrial atmosphere of reciprocal respect and cooperation.

Walter E. Baer

Contents

Chapter 1

Management Rights

The Supreme Court of the United States has indicated that in the absence of a contractual provision limiting or prohibiting his right, an employer may legally discharge an employee for any or no cause, subject only to valid state or federal laws imposing limitations on him. In the case of the *United Steelworkers of America* v. *Warrior & Gulf Navigation Co.*, the Court stated:

> Collective bargaining agreements regulate or restrict the exercise of management functions; they do not oust management from the performance of them. Management hires and fires, pays and promotes, supervises and plans. All these are part of its function, and absent a collective bargaining agreement, it may be exercised freely except as limited by published law and by the willingness of employees to work under the particular, unilaterally imposed conditions. . . .[1]

Actually, the right of an employer to discharge without just cause was a creature of the common law of the nineteenth century. One of the basic purposes of a collective bargaining agreement, at least for the union organization that negotiates it, is to modify this power and require the employer to deal justly with all employees when taking disciplinary or discharge action.

The National Labor Relations Act, the Taft Act, the Fair Employment Practices Act, the veterans' reemployment provisions of the Selective Service Act, and other statutes have all circumscribed the right of employers and the scope of their powers to discharge without

Note. Full citations appear at the end of the book.

1

just cause. The adoption of a collective bargaining agreement by an employer nearly always results in a further narrowing of his discharge powers, irrespective of whether it spells out such restrictions in detail.

CONTRACTUAL TERMS

Provisions

The parties to labor agreements appear to deal with the problem of management's power to discipline and discharge in one or more of three ways.

First, they may adopt a generalized management protection clause that provides an outline and review of the various prerogatives reserved to the employer. Typical of such a clause is one that reads:

> *Recognition of Management:* The Management has the responsibility to direct the operations of the Company and to determine the number and location of its plant or plants and departments therein; the products to be manufactured; the methods, processes, and means of manufacturing; the sources, materials, and supplies; and the disposition of products. The Company also has the right to discipline or discharge any employee for just cause and to transfer and lay off because of lack of work or for other legitimate reasons, provided that none of these functions of the Management shall be exercised so as to abrogate or nullify any specific provision of this Contract. Any dispute arising therefrom shall be taken up and adjusted under the regular grievance procedure.

Second, employers and unions may work out contractual terms relating specifically to discharge and disciplinary cases. The following is a standard example:

> Any employee who has been disciplined by a layoff or a discharge may request the presence of the Shop Steward of his area to discuss the case with him before he is required to leave the plant. The Shop Steward will be called promptly.

> Any employee who is removed from his work and taken to an office for interview may, if he so desires, call the Shop Steward to be present with him during such interview. The Shop Steward, however, will be present only as a witness for the employee, and may negotiate on the matter only after the employee has a grievance as a result of the interview.

> It is important that complaints regarding unjust or discriminatory layoffs or discharges be handled promptly according to the grievance procedure.

Grievances must be filed within forty-eight (48) hours of the layoff or discharge, and the Company will review and render a decision on the case within five (5) working days of its receipt.

If the employee is not found to be unjustly disciplined by layoff or discharge, such layoff or discharge shall be absolute as of the date of such disciplinary action.

If the employee is found to be unjustly disciplined by layoff or discharge, he shall be paid for all time lost and reinstated.

If, after the decision of the Management, the case is not appealed by the Shop Committee within five (5) working days, the matter will be considered closed.

The third form of contractual provision concerns primarily the employer's right to maintain order and efficiency through shop rules or similar devices. A typical clause states:

The rules and regulations of the Company shall continue in full force and effect, and the Company shall have the right to amend such rules and regulations and to make further rules and regulations, provided they are not contrary to the terms of this Agreement and provided that a copy of any amendments or further rules and regulations shall be submitted to the Chairman of the Bargaining Committee twenty-four (24) hours before posting, except in case of emergency.

In 1969 the Bureau of National Affairs reported on contractual provisions in 400 separate labor agreements involving a variety of employers and unions.[2] The study showed that 82 percent of the contracts contained a general statement relative to the grounds for discharge, such as just cause. A total of 21 percent contained an itemization of company rules. Failure to meet work standards was a basis for dismissal in 18 percent of this sampling, a contract violation committed by an employee in 30 percent, and an employee's unauthorized absence—most frequently of three to five days or an "excessive" number of times—in 20 percent.

An examination of these contracts revealed that the parties had agreed on certain procedures for management to follow when it was either contemplating or actually instituting a discharge action. A warning was required before discharge in 7 percent of the cases. The employer was obliged to issue a notice to the employee of the contemplated action in 25 percent of the agreements, with notice to the union required either preceding or following the dismissal in 32 percent of the 400 contracts. In 7 percent, the employee had to have previously been suspended before discharge could be instituted. Union participation in the procedure was required in 6 percent of the contracts, and 9 percent provided for the company to hold hearings or discussions with the employee and/or the union before discharge could be imposed.

Another aspect analyzed was the appeals and grievance machinery designed for the specific purpose of handling discharge cases: special procedures appeared in 8 percent of the agreements. Some contracts stipulated the period within which the discharged employee-grievant and/or the union was required to file a complaint contesting the action. The time limit of one to three days appeared in 23 percent, with 31 percent permitting four to seven days and another 7 percent providing for eight days or more.

Many of these labor agreements made some provision for the handling of cases of discharged employees who were later reinstated. A general statement dealing with this subject appeared in 53 percent of the contracts; 27 percent provided for reinstatement with full back pay and another 7 percent with only limited back pay; and 53 percent allowed for reinstatement at the discretion of an arbitrator.

These figures represent a noticeable increase during the 1960s in the frequency with which just cause for discharge was expressly required in union contracts. The stipulation appeared in 11 percent more of the 400 agreements analyzed in 1969 than in a sample the same size treated in a 1961 survey.[3] More than half the later contracts spelled out discharge procedures. Grounds for dismissal were detailed more frequently in manufacturing than in nonmanufacturing contracts—62 percent as against 43. The causes most often specified were violation of the contract, violation of company rules, incompetence or failure to meet work standards, intoxication, dishonesty or theft, unauthorized or excessive absences, insubordination, and misconduct.

Other grounds that were stated, but much less frequently, included wage garnishments, immoral conduct, narcotics trafficking (maritime industry), bribe taking, and failure to obey safety rules (construction).

An interesting development between the 1961 and 1969 surveys, which may represent a growing trend, involves the contractual statute of limitations under which past offenses are wiped off the disciplinary record book after a specified period. In the later study, such a clause appeared in 17 percent of the agreements—19 percent of the manufacturing and 13 percent of the nonmanufacturing—as compared with the 1961 figures of only 13 and 4 percent respectively.

Exclusions

Although much less frequently found, there are labor agreements that prohibit arbitration review of discipline and discharge actions taken by the employer. These are voluntary issues for collective bargaining, according to an interesting legal separation articulated in a 1958 Supreme Court decision.[4] In it, the Court recognized three distinct categories of bargaining proposals and set down three types of rules regarding them.

1. *Mandatory topics.* Under the Labor Management Relations Act (LMRA), section 8(d), both parties are required to negotiate in good faith with respect to wages, hours, and other conditions of employment. The party submitting such proposals may insist on their inclusion in any contract executed, and the other party is compelled to bargain on them. In this area, bargaining may proceed to an impasse.

2. *Voluntary topics.* Either party may place such topics on the table, hoping for voluntary bargaining and ultimate agreement. However, the receiving party cannot be required either to negotiate on them or to agree on their inclusion in any contract executed. If the advancing party demands their inclusion—in other words, insists on bargaining to an impasse—this constitutes a violation of its bargaining duty under the act.

3. *Illegal topics.* Subjects forbidden under the LMRA would include such things as proposals for a closed shop. Neither party can insist that the other bargain on these topics, and they are improper if later included in the agreement even with the other party's consent.

Where does collective bargaining on discipline and discharge fit into this legal picture? The answer is that an employer must be willing to discuss the issues of discharge and discipline with employees or their representatives. However, the National Labor Relations Board (NLRB) has ruled that an employer did not violate his bargaining duty when he insisted on excluding these issues from the arbitration process. In this significant holding, the Board found that the company was quite willing to discuss its challenged discharge and discipline actions all through the grievance procedure; it insisted only upon *not arbitrating* them. The employer's right to this position was supported by the Board.[5]

A provision excluding arbitration was also contained in a contract between Nassau Inn, Inc. and the Hotel, Motel, Bar and Cafeteria Employees Union. It stated that the right of discharge "is reserved to the employer and in no case would such discharge constitute a grievance or be eligible for arbitration." The bargaining history of this clause revealed that the union had wanted it to call for the submission of summary discharges to both the grievance procedure and arbitration but that the parties had been unable to agree on anything except the employer's unilateral jurisdiction. Customarily, discharge cases are held to be arbitrable almost without fail unless the contract expressly states the contrary, in which case there is no obligation for the parties to seek arbitration. Such was the situation here. The intent of the parties as confirmed in the language and the bargaining history of their agreement left the arbitrator no recourse but to find that the grievance of an employee who was summarily discharged for insubordination was not arbitrable under the contract. Thus holding, he refrained from deciding the case on its merits.[6]

CONTRACTUAL LIMITATIONS

It seems to be a well-established rule of contract administration as handed down in the great majority of arbitral opinions that an employer does not have an unrestricted right to discipline, even though the collective bargaining agreement does not expressly and specifically limit it. In other words, the mere presence of a labor agreement tends to require the employer to act only for cause. The reasoning is that a fundamental purpose of the agreement is to provide the workers with some form of job security. To allow an employer to exercise solely his own discretion in determining the justness of his discipline and discharge actions would render this premise null.

A number of cases from respectable arbitral authority support this conclusion. For example, though dealing with a labor agreement that did not expressly qualify the company's disciplinary power with a just cause requirement, Arbitrator Walter E. Boles evaluated the propriety of the employer's discharge action according to this standard. He founded his argument on the premise that a just cause basis for discipline is implied in an agreement in the absence of a clear proviso to the contrary. In this holding, the arbiter referred to another decision of his, an unpublished one that involved the Southwestern Bell Telephone Company and the Communications Workers of America,[7] and then stated:

> The Arbitrator is fully aware that the Contract between these parties does not contain the conventional "just" or "proper" cause language in connection with disciplinary matters.

But certain realities must be recognized. . . . The first "reality" in the situation is that the Arbitrator must consider this "issue" on the same basis he would use if the Contract provided for "discharge for just cause." Any other approach simply is not realistic [today] . . . (when the bulk of the 100,000 collective bargaining agreements contain "just cause" or comparable language). If parties today do not intend that arbitrators make "just cause" appraisals of disciplinary action, they should so indicate in their writing.[8]

Most managements want and attempt to interpret and administer the labor agreement as though it contained the only limitations on their absolute right to manage the enterprise as they see fit. Under this concept, they are wont to argue that the union's claims must fall unless it can point to a specific contractual provision on which its action is based.

On the other hand, most arbitrators concur in the view that there are too many unforeseeable contingencies for a contract to constitute the sole definition of the privileges accorded to the union and the employees during its term; moreover, with a document only 25 to 75 pages long, there may be inadvertent or even deliberate omissions. The parties may attempt to regulate all aspects of their complicated relationship from the most crucial to the most minor by giving as extensive and comprehensive specifications as they can formulate. But this is not often possible or even practicable because of the compulsion to reach agreement and the breadth of the matters covered as well as the need for a fairly concise and readable instrument. The product of negotiations—the written document—is, in the words of the late Harry Shulman, "a compilation of diverse provisions; some provide objective criteria almost automatically applicable; some provide more or less specific standards which require reason and judgment in their application; and some do little more than leave problems to future considerations with an expression of hope and good faith."[9]

An interesting and peculiar aspect of discipline and discharge controversies is that the parties to labor agreements appear to be much less articulate in drafting the clauses governing such matters than they commonly are on almost all other potential problems. This may be because of the sensitivity to the subject of both sides and their inability or unwillingness to cope with it comprehensively. Employers may refrain from giving it full language coverage in the hope of retaining greater latitude in their decisions. Unions may be motivated by the feeling that the less said explicitly about the subject, the greater will be the question in an arbitrator's mind as to the scope of management's power to act. Although these are only speculations, one thing is certain —the majority of collective bargaining agreements speak far less concretely on discipline and discharge problems than on most other contractual points.

Past Practice

Gaps left in a contract may be filled in by reference to the practices of the particular industry and of the various shops covered by the agreement. An example of the limitations that such precedents can impose on management's power to discharge or discipline is found in a decision by Arbitrator John W. May. The dispute involved a contract that contained no provision relating to the discharge of employees. Over the objections of the company, a union representative reported off from work for union business. Upon his return, the company had a replacement for him. Almost immediately thereafter, the company discharged the union official, alleging that he had caused a strike to take place because he was provoked by the company's action in replacing him. When the union's grievance was argued before the arbitrator, the employer contended that no law or agreement prohibited the company from dismissing an employee. The only mention of discharge in the contract was contained within the union's security provisions dealing with employees' failures to pay union dues. The arbitrator's comments relative to the employer's position and the weight of past practice in the absence of contractual language are worthy of review:

> Under the conditions of no Contract provision to the contrary the Company arrogates [to] itself the right to discharge with or without reason. This is legalism in its most abused form. There is no reason why if the Contract is silent it could not then be interpreted in exactly the reverse form so that the Company would be unable to discharge an employee for any reason. The silence of the Contract could be used in such a way that all discharges are legal except those violative of Federal or State statute. The legal profession has long since recognized that not all incidents are covered by statutory enactment and jurists have developed the law of equity to deal with such cases. An arbitration proceeding is more like equity than statutory law proceedings. We are here lacking a rule of law due to its absence in the Contract and equity must, therefore, prevail.

> Again, reliance must be had [on] past practice, since rules of conduct are lacking in the Agreement. Mr. Edward Bamford testified the Company was responsible in its dealings with its employees and had few discharges in its history, not more than 15 in 30 years of operation. Further,

there was good cause underlying these dismissals, in most cases dishonesty. Herein is the pattern over the past 30 years of discharge for just cause. In the case of X_____, therefore, just cause must also be shown. This cannot be construed as writing in or amending the Contract when a practice has existed for 30 years and serves as a basis for negotiation and agreement.[10]

The Internal Logic of the Contract

A labor agreement contained a statement in the management's rights clause that the employer retained the sole right to discharge. Arbitrator R. H. Morvant held that, though rights may be reserved in this way, this did not mean they were unrestricted. He reasoned that they were expressly qualified by two other provisions of the contract, which provided for loss of seniority and vacation rights upon discharge "for cause" and thus clearly established that management's right was intended to be limited to discharge for cause. It was the employer's argument that the term "for cause" could not be interpreted to mean just or good cause, and he therefore might discharge for any reason without protest. Arbiter Morvant rejected this contention on the ground that it annuls the basic principles of all labor-management agreements. He made the following comments on this point:

> The labor-management agreement reduces to writing the rights of the individual worker and protects those rights against any arbitrary or unfair action on the part of representatives of the company. To agree with the Company that "cause" in this instant case means "any reason" would make meaningless all the rights of the individual worker. If the Company can discharge and not be subject to protest for such unilateral action, it is conceivable that the Company could abrogate all of the provisions of the Agreement, including the wage rates, simply by discharging any employee who dared to protest. Consequently, we must interpret the term "discharge for cause" as denoting a fair and legitimate reason for termination, since such action cuts brutally across the economic life of the person involved.[11]

Other decisions reflect the arbitral viewpoint that each collective bargaining agreement tacitly assumes an employer shall not arbitrarily exercise his power of discharge. Accordingly it has been held that an employer was not free to act without just cause despite the absence of a contract clause stating this.[12] In a dispute at the Atwater Manufacturing Company, for example, the company claimed unlimited discharge powers under a collective bargaining agreement that did not expressly restrict them. A board of three arbitrators rejected this view on the ground that, if the company could discharge without cause, it could also lay off without cause. Further, it could recall, transfer, or promote in violation of seniority provisions simply by invoking its claimed right to discharge. They expressed their rationale in these words:

> A collective bargaining agreement is a comprehensive instrument by virtue of which the parties agree to recognize respective rights. No agreement covers all questions which might arise under its terms and because of this the parties included a grievance procedure and arbitration to resolve questions as to the meaning of the agreement and its application. However, basic to every agreement must be a quality of consistency and logic. Obviously, parties will not by agreement bind themselves to provisions which are contradictory and meaningless. Thus, when one of the parties claims a right which the explicit terms of the agreement either modify or abolish, the claimed right will need strong argument to stand.
>
> In the instant case the Company claims an unlimited right to discharge. The basis of its claim is that the Agreement does not state that the Company does not have the right. The fact is, however, that in the Agreement both the Company and the Union have agreed on definite employee rights, which rights would be meaningless if they did not necessarily imply a severe modification of the Company's right to discharge.
>
> Thus, the explicit terms of the Agreement, by establishing rights which are wholly inconsistent with the claims of the Company, must logically be considered to have modified any claimed rights which are not there expressed and which are inconsistent with the explicit terms of the Agreement.[13]

All the above decisions have a common thread of reasoning running through them: an employer's powers of discharge are curtailed with the birth of the written labor document. Such limitations are an implied term of the contract, created by the necessity for preserving harmony among the contract's component parts.

The question may also arise of whether a company may discipline for a lesser degree of an offense than the contract stipulates. For example, does the use of the term "gross negligence" in a labor agreement prohibit an employer from discharging an employee for *ordinary* negligence? That was one of the issues facing James V. Altieri in settling a dispute between the Brewer Dry Dock Company and the Brewer Dry Dock Employees Association Inc. The agreement stated that the employer retained the right to "discipline an employee for violation of rules or other proper cause," and "proper cause" might be "drunkenness or insubordination, or habitual taking of days off, or gross negligence, or theft from fellow employees or from the company, or fighting or gambling on company property." Although the union conceded that employees could properly be found guilty of ordinary negligence, the company could not invoke the discharge clause because it defined only *gross* negligence as proper cause for disciplinary action, so that by implication ordinary negligence was excluded. The arbiter disagreed. He was of the opinion that the examples of proper cause listed in the contract were not intended to be complete or exclusive but illustrative only, so as to eliminate from dispute the question of whether the conduct described warranted disciplinary action.[14]

EMPLOYEES' RIGHTS IN AN INTERIM PERIOD

Some companies have discovered, probably much to their chagrin, that individual employee contract rights may govern their discharge decisions after an existing collective bargaining agreement has expired. Such has been the holding by both arbitrators and courts. According to one court's finding, the terms and conditions of a collective bargaining agreement provide rights that establish a standard for the individual employment contract embracing each worker that comes into operation upon the expiration of the collective bargaining instrument.[15]

Court decisions take into account any actions of the employer during the period between the expiration of the agreement and the commencement of the negotiated instrument that follows it. The investigation traces the character of the interim relationship between the parties to determine whether they intended to conduct it in keeping with terms that had outlived the prior agreement.

Where an employer has taken steps to establish new conditions governing the relationship in the interim period, the courts have ruled differently. For example, an employee was laid off during the term of a contract that contained a seniority clause entitling him to reinstatement. Before his reinstatement, the contract expired. The court in this case held that labor agreements do not "extend rights created and arising under the contract beyond its life, when it has been terminated in accordance with its provisions," and that the "rights of the parties to work under the contract are fixed by the contract" and "persist during [and] end with its term."[16]

When the contract expired, the company had posted rules that defined the employment relationships with the workers for the interim period during which no collective bargaining agreement existed. Subsequently, it entered into a labor agreement with the union. In this instance, neither the posted rules nor the later negotiated instrument provided the laid-off employee protection of his seniority rights. Therefore, no implied individual contract could be presumed that maintained the stipulations in the expired agreement: the employees' acceptance of the company-established rules and the later negotiated instrument produced express contracts that governed the relationships during both these periods.

Arbitral opinion has held that individual employment contracts arise by implication where a collective bargaining agreement has expired and the union and the employer have failed to sign a new contract. The rationale behind this stand closely follows the reasoning in court decisions on such cases. In one dispute, the employer had not notified the employees of the terms under which they would continue to work—that is, the terms of the individual contract that would prevail—after the previously negotiated agreement had expired. The arbiter ruled that the provisions and exclusions of the collective instrument were still applicable to the people it had covered and thus governed the individual employer-employee relationship. The expired agreement had contained no specification of mandatory retirement age; accordingly, the company was held not to have just cause to discharge an employee on the ground that he had reached 65.[17]

Through a range of cases, then, arbitral and court opinion has considered management's prerogatives—whether expressed in the contract or implied as residual rights—to be qualified by the necessity that they be fair and reasonable rather than capricious or arbitrary. A company's inherent right to set and maintain workable standards of behavior for employees is counterbalanced by the presumption that it will exercise its authority and judgment equitably.

THE ESTABLISHMENT OF RULES

Under its general rights article, management usually reserves the right to establish rules and procedures governing the conduct of its employees. The typical clause of this kind states that management may issue and promulgate such directives provided they are reasonable and do not establish conditions that may constitute a violation of the contract. This is commonly the limit of the language. However, a minority of labor agreements have actually outlined the specific rules, either including them among the contractual provisions that have been negotiated and agreed on or specifying that they will be unilaterally established by the employer as a function of the rights reserved to management. An even smaller number of labor agreements contain both the actual rules and regulations agreed on and the steps to be taken, including the penalties to be imposed in the event of infractions.

The existence of some rules is essential to the orderly operation of any enterprise. A company is analogous to a small society. Just as the whole of society requires laws for its own well-being and for the protection of its citizens, so does the firm need rules and regulations aimed at furthering its interests and insuring the health, safety, and welfare of its employees. Since the primary responsibility for the operation of the enterprise rests with the management, it must have the authority to establish reasonable rules and to discipline and discharge if it is to meet its obligations to the owners, stockholders, and employees.

The labor agreement normally outlines the essential negotiated terms and conditions of employment that will govern the relationship of the parties for a prescribed period. The residual rights theory holds that all powers not limited or denied to a company by a contractual provision are reserved to management. It is not unheard of for a labor agreement to impose some restriction on the employer's right to issue rules and regulations, but this is very rare. In the absence of such a provision, the parties are generally assumed to have concurred that the employer is to deal with disciplinary matters and will do so reasonably and with sound discretion. The reserved rights theory constitutes a well-established and widely applied principle in interpretations of collective bargaining agreements and is supported by the overwhelming weight of respected arbitral opinion.

The Test of Applicability

Most rules are promulgated by employers to produce orderly employee behavior that will result in an efficient and productive operation. Therefore, they are primarily anticipatory, intended to head off problems before they occur. However, some rules develop to cover situations the employer had not foreseen. Occasionally these are prompted by the improper behavioral stance of a small group of employees. Unions have been known to challenge the reasonableness of such a restriction on the contention that it was discriminatory—that a rule designed to prevent abuses by a comparatively small percentage of employees is unfair to the properly behaving majority.

Managements have always found that most employees are conscientious and honest and are quite willing to comply with any reasonable rules made necessary by the employment relationship. Despite this fact, an employer is not prohibited from imposing a general requirement on even those workers who might not be tempted to behave improperly without it. Certainly it should not be necessary, and arbitrators so hold, for an industrial situation to become unmanageable because of widespread employee misconduct before the company may take reasonable steps to curtail it. The essence of every shop rule and disciplinary regulation is general and uniform applicability.

The Test of Reasonableness

Management's established rules must be reasonable both in context and in administration. A rule that is appropriate in one industrial situation may on its face be quite inappropriate in another. For example, prohibiting smoking is eminently fair and reasonable in a factory where the danger of fire and explosion is great, but it is not where such dangers do not exist. Or the nature of the operations may make absenteeism and moonlighting more critical problems in one industrial situation than in another. Moreover, a just rule can be unjustly implemented—by management's requiring too strict adherence, for example, or imposing overly severe penalties for infractions.

For these reasons, a union customarily reserves to itself the right to challenge company rules and disciplinary actions. Management's decisions are then subject to review under the contract's grievance and arbitration provisions. In these forums, a company's action is appraised in the light of the agreement to determine whether the action was fair and reasonable, whether the right employee was its subject, and whether he was in fact guilty of the alleged infraction.

Safety precautions may be put to the test of reasonableness on the basis of exactly opposing complaints—that they are too lax or that they are too burdensome. Most contracts place on the company the responsibility of making reasonable efforts to provide safe and healthful working conditions. Unfortunately, a good many employers fail to meet their obligations to the best of their ability. Grievances in this area are still far too numerous. Occasionally, however, a dedicated management will find itself charged by the union with overzealousness. The Bethlehem Steel Corporation issued a rule requiring all employees, except when working in offices, to wear hard hats and safety glasses at all times. The union filed a general grievance contending that the rule constituted a contractual violation. It did not object to the accouterments under many circumstances. After asserting that the company was in violation by failing to secure its prior agreement on the rule, the union alleged that requiring all employees to use these safety articles at all times was not reasonable or necessary.

The arbitrator's ruling made three points. First, under the contract, the company had the exclusive power to issue safety rules, and the union's function was confined to cooperation with and joint review of the safety program. Second, the rule bore a reasonable relationship to the employer's safety objectives. Third, the company's administration of the rule would be limited by a contractual provision that precluded discipline except for just cause.[18]

Here is an instance of a rule that is reasonable on its face but whose supervisory administration may be adjudged unreasonable. Its application would scarcely be just if an employee were disciplined for re-moving the hard hat while taking a shower or answering a call of nature or for taking off steamed safety glasses to clean them. By up-holding the company's right to promulgate such a rule and finding the rule reasonable, the arbiter did not pass on any discipline that might be imposed in individual cases. Each disciplinary action taken by the company would have to stand on its own merits and meet the test of just cause.

One employer determined it must do something to control excessive absenteeism. The labor agreement expressly gave it the right to make, publish, and enforce reasonable plant rules that did not conflict with the agreement. The union tested the reasonableness of the company's decision that it could discipline and discharge employees for excused as well as unexcused absences. The arbiter held that when an em-ployee had requested and received management's permission to be off, it could not consider him to have committed an offense, and that penalizing him as though he had was contrary to the contractual re-quirement of just cause for discipline. The decision, therefore, was that the administration of the rule was unreasonable.[19]

There is a long line of arbitration cases, on the other hand, where the decision has gone the other way. Certainly no business can func-tion efficiently and profitably without a constant and reliable work-force. Excessive absences interfere with work schedules, necessitate replacements and additional manpower, and cause substantial losses of time and money. Therefore, although an employee's absences may be for valid reasons, they may still be considered excessive and unaccept-able. Obviously a valid excuse will be of small consolation to an em-ployer when the employee's productive effort is frequently unavailable.

Thus many arbiters have held that when an individual is absent so often over a continuing period, even excusably and justifiably, that he is of little value and perhaps is actually a hindrance to the company, it may eventually terminate the employment relationship. Most often such an action is considered to constitute a nondisciplinary discharge.[20]

The reasonableness of a rule that provided for a monetary levy on employees who lost tools through negligence was the issue between Aro, Inc. (Arnold Air Force Station, Tennessee) and the International Association of Machinists. Arbitrator George Savage King held that the company had not violated the contract by adopting the rule. The agreement recognized the employer's right to adopt and enforce reasonable rules and regulations for efficient operations. The provision implied that enforcement could be produced through disciplinary action. The arbiter concluded that this contract gave the company the right to deduct from pay checks under the proper circumstances for lost tools, and he deemed the rule reasonable in that employees were charged only for *negligent* loss.[21]

Again we have a rule considered reasonable on its face and necessary because of serious potential operational difficulties and expenses. However, the administration of the rule was another matter. The company did not carry the burden of showing that an employee's loss of a tool was in fact caused by negligence. Instead, it relied entirely on his not reporting the loss before inventory investigations revealed it. The arbiter concluded that the employee might simply not know the tool was missing. The company did not require employees to make frequent inventories of their tools. Equally important, it gave them no opportunity to explain losses. Certainly it was incumbent on management to determine whether a given situation involved negligence. The arbiter recommended that a standardized procedure for soliciting the employees' explanation would help a great deal to establish that the application of the rule was reasonable.

The Test of Sufficient Publicizing

In society at large, ignorance of the law generally constitutes no excuse. The citizen who alleges ignorance to defend his violation of a given law is seldom excused by law-enforcement people. A somewhat different condition exists in industrial society: arbitrators have customarily held that an employee cannot be expected to comply with rules and regulations he does not know. One arbiter has stated:

> In matters of criminal law, all persons are deemed to know it, but in the area of labor-management discipline, employees are not bound to know particular rules, although it is true that serious misconduct may be the

subject of disciplinary action, even in the absence of specific regulation. Just cause requires that employees be informed of a rule [whose] infraction . . . may result in suspension or discharge, unless conduct is so clearly wrong that specific reference is not necessary.[22]

Rarely have arbiters upheld a management's attempt to discipline an employee for violating a rule that was not published or adequately promulgated. The employee's ignorance of it constitutes a sustainable defense if he can establish that he could not have known it. This is why some employers have chosen to enumerate their factory rules and regulations fully and prominently within the covers of the labor document. Still others publish them in an employee handbook, which, in addition, generally outlines other conditions or benefits in the employment relationship. The majority seem to prefer to use bulletin boards scattered throughout the operating facility. In any case, a management will find it extremely difficult to have a disciplinary action sustained by an arbitrator unless it can establish that it has taken steps to communicate its rules effectively.

Furthermore, it is usually advisable not to impose penalties for the infraction of a rule instantly following its publication. Most employers have found it better to issue the rule, advise employees of the date it will go into effect (perhaps one week later), and state that violations occurring thereafter will result in disciplinary penalties. This alerts the employees to management's position and enables them to make any necessary preparations for compliance with the rule.

Review and Consent by the Union

It is usually a good procedure for the employer to discuss new or revised plant rules with union officers before communicating them to the employees. This is merely a courtesy under a labor agreement that does not impose a contractual obligation on the employer to inform the union before issuing rules. On the other hand, advance communication may be necessary where there is a contractual provision on the subject.

For example, the McCord Corporation unilaterally instituted a rule requiring employees to clock in and out at lunch time for the purpose, it maintained, of improving administrative control. The union contested this action on the ground that the company was contractually prohibited from instituting what the union described as a new rule without first consulting it and getting its consent. The employer contended that such advance discussions were only a matter of business courtesy. The arbitrator did not wholly concur with either view. He held that the contract gave the employer the right to institute plant rules covering employee conduct so long as they did not violate the terms of the contract and were not used to discriminate against employees because of union membership. However, a supplemental agreement specifically excluding plant rules from the collective bargaining instrument obliged the employer to discuss new rules with the union—though not to obtain its consent—before putting them into effect. Thus the union should have been advised of the rule in advance.[23]

In another case, the United Baking Company unilaterally drew up a complete set of plant and work rules. Although some of the posted rules fell into areas in which the company might act on its own, others involved wages, hours, and working conditions, about which the contract required it to bargain with the union. So finding, the arbitrator ruled that he had no alternative under the agreement but to declare that the entire set of rules was invalid.[24]

Revisions

Arbitral opinion regarding revisions in existing rules is influenced by two factors. The first is the conditions of employment that the rule change will encompass. Thus a revision that directly affects the size of work crews, the amount of pay, or another question basic to the employment relationship is accepted less often than one dealing with a peripheral matter such as safety rules, work clothing, or a procedure intended to improve operating efficiency. The second factor is the weight of past practice. Unions commonly raise past practice as a defense when management attempts to impose a rule change that will reduce a benefit or condition previously enjoyed by the employees.

However, in the majority of instances, if the revision does not negatively affect the negotiable areas expressly addressed in the contract, most arbitrators will allow it on the ground that management has the same reserved right to revise rules as it has to issue them.

In disputes in which the union uses past practice to counter an employer-established rule or a revision, the employer will typically parry with the reserved rights argument that it has the power to promulgate rules or change them. Any rule that threatens the negotiated security derived from existing wages, hours, and working conditions is particularly worrisome to the union and usually meets with vigorous resistance from it.

One such provocative area involves the production standards that employees are expected to satisfy in the performance of their tasks.

When these are the subject of a controversy, it is more common for the employer than the union to rely on past practice to support its position. For example, the National Lead Company of Ohio had a long-standing labor agreement under which it had established production quotas for employees in the machining unit. During the term of the agreement, it instituted time and motion studies and other scientific tests looking toward a revision of the standards. When the tests were completed, employees were notified of new quotas and the amount of production to be expected from each worker. No incentive system was involved here; employees were paid on hourly rate, and each was assigned a certain number of pieces or parts to produce during each shift of work, failing which he could be liable to a disciplinary procedure. The union challenged the employer's right to set such standards.

There was no question before the arbitrator as to whether the standards were fair or unfair. The contract recognized management's right to adopt and enforce reasonable rules and regulations for efficient operations, and the employer was supported by the weight of past practice in that previous production quotas had been unilaterally established without complaint from the union. Arbitrator Carl R. Schedler therefore ruled that the employer had the right to set new standards unilaterally and to impose disciplinary penalties for failure or refusal to meet the quotas.[25]

It is not uncommon for a labor agreement to contain no provision that specifically authorizes or prohibits the establishment of production standards, though in this event other clauses may implicitly recognize this right. A statement in the contract that the management of the plant, and the direction of the workforce, is vested exclusively in the company, for example, would constitute such an acknowledgment in the view of most arbitrators, provided that the company did not invoke this implied right for the purpose of circumventing any other contractual provision.

For this reason, despite the fact that the past practice at the Mead Corporation had been for employees to set their own work standards and take lunch and rest periods whenever they pleased, Arbitrator George E. Strong upheld the employer's right to regulate these matters. He denied the grievance of the United Mine Workers of America, District 50, for the following reasons: (1) the union had been put on notice that the company was contemplating ways to reduce idle time and the establishment of formal and specific standards; (2) there was no evidence that the new standards were unreasonable or that the employees were overworked; (3) no inference could be found that the parties intended the existing loose, imprecise, and informal measurements of a reasonable day's work to become the norm; (4) the employer had made time- and effort-saving changes in operating conditions, equipment, location of materials and lavatory, and accessibility of the lunch wagon; (5) each change had been made to correct inefficient or unreasonable operations; and (6) the contract specifically stated that the employer's failure to exercise a right would not be considered a waiver of that right.[26]

A word of caution is in order here regarding rules governing production standards. It is inadvisable for quotas to be set on an individual employee basis. Arbitrators have held that management can set a standard of proper production only for a *job*. They have also held that where an employee was producing at a rate considered satisfactory for other employees, although perhaps not equal to his previous better effort, the employer was wrong in imposing a disciplinary penalty on him.[27]

STATUTORY LIMITATIONS

In its administration of the Labor Management Relations Act, the National Labor Relations Board has distinguished between "unlawful" employee activities, which are expressly barred by the unfair practices provisions of the LMRA, and "unprotected" activities, which are not expressly banned. The Board has held that employees engaging in concerted action that is found to be unprotected forfeit their rights under the LMRA and thus cannot successfully obtain reinstatement through the NLRB if they are discharged for such action.[28]

One court has said that an employee "may be discharged . . . for a good reason, a poor reason, or no reason at all, so long as the terms of the LMRA statute are not violated." [29]

Stating this opinion even more specifically, the U.S. Supreme Court has said that the act "permits a discharge for any reason other than union activity or agitation for collective bargaining." [30]

Putting it another way, a third court has said, "The question is not whether the discharges were related or unrelated, just or unjust, nor whether as disciplinary measures they were mild or drastic. These are matters to be determined by management." This court commented that the sole duty of the National Labor Relations Board was to determine whether the discharges had the purposes of discouraging or encouraging union membership or taking reprisals against employees for engaging in concerted activities protected under the law.[31]

Federal Laws

The most significant statutory limitation on management's right to discipline or discharge is section 8(a)(3) of the Labor-Management Relations Act, which makes it an unfair labor practice for an employer "by discriminating in regard to . . . tenure of employment to encourage or discourage membership in any labor organization." Further, section 8(a)(4) forbids a management "to discharge or otherwise discriminate against an employee because he has filed charges or given testimony under this Act." The Fair Labor Standards Act (FLSA) likewise protects employees who facilitate the enforcement of the law. Under section 15(a)(3), it is illegal to discharge or discriminate against employees who institute actions under the law or testify in proceedings. The question of whether a discharge was actually motivated by such a reason is determined by the same kinds of tests that are applied in deciding whether an employer was imposing a penalty for union activity.

Legislation not related to management-labor relations may contain special clauses bearing on employees' rights. For example, section 9(c) of the Universal Military Training and Service Act states that veterans who are restored to their former positions after honorable discharge from the armed forces cannot be discharged without cause within one year.

Another provision of the LMRA, section 8(a)(1), makes it unlawful for an employer to interfere with the right of employees to engage in concerted activities for the purpose of mutual aid or protection. It is significant to employers that the NLRB may consider a discharge to violate this provision even though there is no evidence of union activities and no proof of unlawful motivation on the employer's part. Management must be cautious in taking disciplinary action against any employee who appears to be the communicator of fellow workers' complaints regarding wages, hours, or working conditions. It is not necessary for an actual labor organization to be involved. The employee who acts as a spokesman for his peers, whether he is self-appointed or otherwise, is engaged in "concerted activity," which is protected under federal labor laws. Although the employer may not be required to actually negotiate with a group (or its spokesman) unless evidence is shown that it represents a majority of the employees in a unit appropriate for collective bargaining, he is prohibited under the law from discharging the members for their group activity.

Management's primary concern is that the enterprise function as efficiently as possible. In order to accomplish this objective, it must sometimes take disciplinary or discharge action against employees for insubordination, inefficiency, or troublemaking. In the light of the federal labor statutes protecting employees' rights to join or organize unions and to take part in other concerted actions with legitimate aims, the employer must be constantly on guard not to confuse unacceptable behavior on the job with pursuits that are sanctioned by the law. The dividing line between protected and unprotected activity is indistinct; a review of pertinent NLRB cases demonstrates that the decisions do not follow a hard and fast pattern. In other words, what the NLRB will consider indefensible union conduct and what it will find to be legitimate—although perhaps overexuberant —concerted activity is not always predictable.

In all such disputes, it is the task of the National Labor Relations Board to determine whether the employer's motive in discharging the employee was to punish him for his union activity.

In addition to the unpredictability of any Board decision, another factor the employer must consider carefully is that a ruling against its discharge action can prove very expensive. Besides the cost of mounting a defense before the NLRB, the company may also have to assume the burden of a large back pay award. Such disputes do not move speedily through the Board's slow machinery; they may take many months and even years. If the Board ultimately finds in the employee's favor, back pay will have grown large during this time. Naturally, the employee is supposed to seek other employment actively. But even if he succeeds in locating other work, the company may still have to. make up the difference between his pay on the new job and what he would have received if he had not been discharged.[32]

Certain employee activities may result in the removal of the limitations that the LMRA imposes on the employer's right to discipline or discharge. This occurs in situations where employees have engaged in conduct that the act either specifies to be unlawful, such as a secondary boycott, or merely does not protect, such as an employee strike in violation of a no-strike clause under a labor agreement.

Discrimination Cases

A number of factors are always considered and reviewed by the National Labor Relations Board when it is conducting its investigation to determine whether a discharge was illegal under federal labor laws. It will be seeking answers to a number of questions; and if an employer who is involved in such a dispute answers them honestly to himself, he may be able to judge how successful he will be in his dealings with the Board:

1. What is the company's attitude toward unions generally? What is its attitude toward the union involved in the dispute?
2. What is its attitude toward the individual who has been discharged? Was it aware that the employee was a union member, advocate, or officer? What was the employer's relationship with the individual when he was functioning in a representative capacity?
3. Was a reason for discharge given to the employee when the action was taken? Was the same reason given at that time as is now provided?
4. What is the company's actual reason for discharging the employee? Does the evidence point toward this, or is there evidence that suggests some other motive could have been involved? Was the reason given in writing? If it was given orally, can the employer substantiate precisely what was said?
5. Has the company applied the same penalty to other workers who were guilty of the same offense? Has the rule been enforced consistently?
6. Was the rule communicated fully to the employees, and did it establish a clear policy regarding discharge actions?

If the employer's rule has not been enforced uniformly, the odds are against his being able to show that any discharge was not discriminatory. His problems will be compounded if the rule has not been generally disseminated or has been newly promulgated. On the contrary, the Board has been known to uphold the discharge of a union president when it was shown that he had violated a rule applied equally and impartially to all employees. However, a discharge for stealing company gasoline was ruled discriminatory by the Board when it appeared that it was a common offense not usually penalized.[33]

A discharge occurring shortly after an employee's participation in a union activity is always suspect. In such an instance, the Board will examine very carefully the reasons given by the employer. An example of this is a case where the company claimed there was less need for the work done by the laid-off employee. The Board scrutinized this allegation with the greatest care and learned that others had been hired to do the work following the layoff of the employee. The employer's defense immediately fell.[34]

This does not mean that the timing of a discharge or layoff is proof of discrimination. Timing is only circumstantial evidence, which can be overcome by proof that the reasons given for the action are proper. A company that discharged a union official on the same day he openly distributed union authorization cards was able to have its action supported by showing that the discharge was based on the employee's failure to obey safety regulations and that the decision had been made at an earlier date.

Other circumstances are likely to be considered evidence that a discharge or layoff is discriminatory. These are particularly relevant if the employee is a union member or has led a concerted activity intended for the benefit of fellow workers. Here are some typical examples.

A management discharged several workers and at the same time increased the wages and improved the benefits of other employees in an attempt to defeat unionization.[35] The Board found evidence of discrimination in another case when employees were discharged without any prior warning that this penalty could result from the conduct alleged as the cause of the discharge.[36] The same finding was brought when a company imposed discharges despite a serious labor shortage.[37]

In another case, the Board considered the taint of discrimination present when management discharged employees who had refused to help the company fight union activity.[38] When a company retained nonunion workers and later filled the jobs of discharged union members by hiring new people, the Board found the employer's actions discriminatory.[39] And more than one case has shown that when an employer questions an employee regarding union membership, puts him under surveillance to determine whether he attends union meetings, and then in this contaminated atmosphere discharges him or lays him off, there are already two strikes against the company that is charged with discrimination.[40]

Chapter 2

Just Cause

The 1969 survey by the Bureau of National Affairs discussed in Chapter 1 revealed that 82 percent of the 400 representative contracts expressly stipulated some grounds for discharge. A general statement that discharge could be made for "just cause" or "cause" appeared in 71 percent of the agreements. Many of them also stated one or more specific grounds, but few attempted to include a complete listing of actionable offenses or indicated the penalty for particular violations. This is one reason that discharge and discipline continue to be the issues most frequently submitted to arbitration. Disputes are constantly being tested by unions through contractual grievance procedures, and in the majority of instances, a case is ultimately appealed to an impartial arbitrator.

Arbiters are indispensable agents in a peaceful collective bargaining process. Their responsibility is to determine whether the draftsmen of the contract have included or excluded a particular issue from arbitral review and, if included, what the specific remedy should be. The arbitrator is limited to interpreting and applying the collective instrument. His role is not to dispense his own brand of industrial justice; as the Supreme Court has said, "He may of course look for guidance from many sources, yet his award is legitimate only so long as it draws its essence from the collective bargaining agreement. When the arbitrator's words manifest an infidelity to this obligation, courts have no choice but to refuse enforcement of the award." [1]

The Court also said, in the *United Steelworkers of America* v. *Warrior & Gulf Navigation Co.* case, that section 301 of the LMRA assigns to the courts the duty of determining whether the reluctant party has breached his promise to arbitrate. On this point, it stated that arbitration "is a matter of contract and a party cannot be required to submit to arbitration any dispute which he has not agreed so to submit." [2] Thus discipline and discharge cases are excluded from arbitral review if the contractual language clearly and explicitly bars them. But the wording must be unmistakable, since the Court also held that matters should be considered susceptible to arbitration unless expressly excluded.

However, an examination of the 400 labor agreements surveyed in 1969 reveals that the great majority do provide for arbitral consideration of discipline and discharge disputes. Therefore, the meaning of the term "just cause" or "cause," which appears in 71 percent of the contracts, becomes a factor of substantial import to both parties in their collective bargaining arrangement.

Before exploring the meaning of just cause in the minds of various arbitrators, let us glance briefly at agreements that merely state that a discharge must be for cause. The unqualified term "cause" has produced conflicting arbitration opinions regarding the precise nature of this limitation on management's right to discharge. There are arbitrators who have taken the view that, by using the single word "cause," the parties must have envisioned a more inflexible standard than would be entailed by the broader term "just cause." [3] On the other hand, some have equated "cause" with "just cause" or with the standard of "reasonable" and "sufficient" justification. The single word has also been interpreted as intending a "fair and legitimate reason," not merely "any reason." [4]

DEFINITIONS OF JUST CAUSE

What is "just cause"? The answer to this question has been somewhat mystifying to management representatives and union officials; it has even proved elusive to arbitrators. A reading of arbitral opinion produces no standardized definition. Usually the parties to an agreement containing a just cause condition do not give an arbitrator much help on what they consider to be just and fair. This forces him to follow his own judgment, and of course one individual's concepts may differ substantially from another's. Moreover, as one member of the profession has said, in determining just cause where an agreement vests management with the right to discipline, an arbitrator should not substitute his own judgment for management's unless he finds that the employer acted arbitrarily, unreasonably, or in bad faith. [5]

The decisions of arbitrators are final and binding rulings on only the particular dispute decided; as one opinion expressed it, "What constitutes just cause is a matter that must be based on the individual merits of each case." [6] Its outcome will be determined by the facts and circumstances involved in it and the contractual language of the agreement. Such factors as past practice, the history of negotiations between the parties, and the skill of the respective advocates at the hearing table will also be influential. For the most part, arbitrators feel at liberty to disregard colleagues' rulings on other cases, though they will examine these for guidance. Decisions that deal with comparable contractual situations show them the reasoning behind other respected arbitral opinions. It is from this source that arbitrators have formed their general conclusions on what constitutes just and proper cause for discipline and discharge under a labor agreement.

Some Arbitral Views on Just Cause

Under one company's contract, management had reserved to itself the complete function of discharging employees. The only protection afforded employees was the statement that "A discharge may not be arbitrary or capricious or without just cause." The arbiter joined his colleagues in the frustrating search for a key to the enigma of what just cause is. He finally remarked:

> About all that an impartial Arbitrator can do, therefore, is to decide the justice or injustice of the discharge here in question in the light of (a) common sense, (b) common knowledge of generally prevailing industry standards for employee deportment and (c) common understanding of . . . absent specific criteria mutually agreed on [whereby] an Employer may fairly and justly discharge an employee with seniority rights.[7]

Arbitrator Harry H. Platt, a highly respected authority in the arbitration profession, decided a case between the Steelworkers and the Riley Stoker Corp. in which the definition of just cause was at issue. Arbitrator Platt's comments in this case have often been referred to by labor practitioners in their search for a meaningful concept:

> It is ordinarily the function of an arbitrator in interpreting a contract provision which requires "sufficient cause" as a condition precedent to discharge not only to determine whether the employee involved is guilty of wrongdoing and, if so, to confirm the employer's right to discipline where its exercise is essential to the objective of efficiency, but also [to] safeguard the interests of the discharged employee by making reasonably

sure that the causes for discharge were just and equitable and such as would appeal to reasonable and fair-minded persons as warranting discharge. To be sure, no standards exist to aid an arbitrator in finding a conclusive answer to such a question and, therefore, perhaps the best he can do is to decide what reasonable men, mindful of the habits and customs of industrial life and of the standards of justice and fair dealing prevalent in the community, ought to have done under similar circumstances and in that light to decide whether the conduct of the discharged employee was defensible and the disciplinary penalty just.[8]

Another arbitrator has listed the following criteria to guide him in determining whether a discharge is based on a just or reasonable cause:

1. There must be reasonable cause at the time of the discharge. Thus the employer may not justify a discharge based on arbitrary or capricious considerations by referring to subsequent developments.
2. It cannot be said that a disciplinary action has been based on reasonable cause if management searches for justifying reasons after taking the action.
3. Reasonable cause must rest on a valid type of employee failure, not on his job relationship with the employer and not on the company's preferences or predilections.
4. The search for reasonable cause ordinarily may not intrude on an employee's personal life.[9]

In deciding a case between the Electric Hose & Rubber Company and the United Rubber Workers Union, Arbitrator Irvine L. H. Kerrison listed what he judged to be acceptable criteria for evaluating the justness of a penalty of discharge or suspension:

One criterion is that of equal treatment. While this does not mean that all must be judged by the same standards interpreted as giving the same penalties for the same offenses at all times, regardless of extenuating circumstances, it does mean that all must be judged by the same standards as such, and that rules must apply equally to all.

A second criterion is what often is called the rule of reason. Where even, as is not the case here, a Contract does not contain a specific provision protecting employees against unjust discharge or suspension, the Contract as a whole may be held to afford that protection and to challenge any company procedure that threatens to unjustly deprive employees of rights and privileges contained within the four corners of that document.

A third criterion is what often is called the test of internal consistency. Whether a company disciplines on a case-by-case basis, or compiles a code of standard violations with appropriate penalties for each, the test is whether or not the pattern of enforcement is consistent.

A fourth criterion is that guilt is personal. The fact that two or more employees are involved in the same act of misconduct does not necessarily justify the same penalty for all. For one thing, the prior disciplinary record of each involved employee often is considered.[10]

Carroll R. Daugherty has developed seven criteria that he has set forth and applied in a number of published decisions on discipline cases. The stature of this arbitrator makes these standards particularly noteworthy. They are embodied in seven questions.

1. Did the employee have foreknowledge that his conduct would be subject to discipline, including possible discharge?
2. Was the rule he violated reasonably related to the safe, efficient, and orderly operation of the company's business?
3. Did the company make a reasonable effort before disciplining him to discover whether he in fact did violate this rule?
4. Was its investigation fair and objective?
5. Did it obtain substantial evidence that the employee was guilty of the offense with which he was charged?
6. Was its decision nondiscriminatory?
7. Was the degree of discipline given him reasonably related to the seriousness of his proven offense and/or to his record with the company? [11]

Although a number of other arbitral opinions are reviewed in this chapter, Carroll Daugherty's carefully reasoned standards are the most comprehensive and yet succinct. For an employer's discipline or discharge to be upheld, all seven questions must be answered in the affirmative. If any one question evokes a negative response, the company's action will either fall or be amended.

The Complexity of the Problem

It will be noted that certain standards are shared by arbitrators, though one may give greater weight to a certain point than do others. Also, some have articulated their criteria more thoroughly and scientifically than have others. This is one factor that contributes to the enigma of just cause—no universal formulas guide management in establishing and implementing discipline policies. Another factor is the silent treatment accorded the subject in a majority of labor agreements. As mentioned before, many contracts do not contain a list of the rules whose violation will produce discipline, and most do not specify the penalties for infractions.

Some employers pursue the concept of "corrective discipline." Intrinsic in this concept is the requirement that each worker be given a fair, objective appraisal and just treatment when a penalty is being imposed. In this connection, management weighs such matters as the individual's length of service and prior work and discipline records in determining what penalty to assess. This alone makes each case an independent one that turns on the particular facts of the situation and the circumstances surrounding it.

When we add to a problem that is already as complex as this the factor of an outside third party, the arbitrator, with his particular intellectual and psychological makeup, we have pulled together most of the ingredients that produce the enigma of just cause. If for no other reason than self-defense, management should strive always to utilize a standard of good and sufficient cause in providing its workers with their deserved full measure of industrial justice.

The Need for a Sound Standard

To a union and other workers, the worth of a standard of just cause cannot be exaggerated. The union recognizes full well that if the employer has an unlimited right to discharge at will, many important contractual provisions are negated. The seniority provisions of the labor agreement presumably insure an orderly procedure for layoff and recall, but a company allowed to discharge at will without cause can easily ignore this contractual machinery merely by firing the employee. The company can thus nullify one of the fundamental benefits the worker derives from the contractual relationship: security in his employment status.

The compelling value of the just cause concept to employees can readily be seen when the results of its absence are contemplated. The security and other benefits of a specific job are only a few of the relevant considerations. Discharge has sometimes been referred to, perhaps a little overdramatically, as the capital punishment of the labor-management relationship. Certainly the general economic climate has a great bearing on how seriously a worker is affected by a discharge. When the economy is strong and levels of unemployment are low, he can usually obtain another job. Also, good skills will help him find suitable employment that will maintain his basic life style. Moreover, if his job tenure has been relatively brief, the break in service and the resultant loss of accumulated seniority and other benefits may be only a small sacrifice to him. However, the impact of a discharge can be severe if the worker possesses many years of service, does not have substantial skills, and finds himself jobless at a time when the general economy is on a downturn.

In any case, everyone experiences an unpleasant psychological reaction to discharge, an action that carries with it a most unfavorable stigma. No matter what the actual circumstances, he realizes that it represents failure on his part in the eyes of a good many of his neighbors and friends. Often he will feel this way himself and must bear it within his own family. He knows too that each time he seeks employment, he must undergo the embarrassment of relating how he lost his prior job.

Although management will likely contest a depiction of discharge as equivalent to capital punishment, it will have to admit that such an action represents the severest penalty it can inflict on its workers and that it always creates a hardship, often quite a critical one. Adding all these factors to the several that were previously mentioned provides a sufficient chronicle of the need unions have to include a just cause concept in their agreements.

The standard of just cause came into being primarily under the influence of unions. For many years before the advent of unionization, management's authoritarian approach to maintaining order and handling personnel intimidated the workingman. Employees will no longer tolerate this treatment, and a management that attempted to practice it would only find itself on a collision course with them. Today employers generally recognize that workers are human beings first and clock-card numbers second. Supervisors have learned that issuing directives supported by valid reasons will obtain more positive reactions than handing down commands and that the industrial philosophy of encouraging self-discipline will be much more effective in the long run than will threats and intimidation. The standard of just cause serves as another measure of security, helping insure that management will give employees fair and equal treatment.

THE SILENT CONTRACT AND JUST CAUSE

Arbitrators are divided on the question of what criteria to follow in evaluating discipline and discharge actions under a contract that makes no mention of any standards. Although there does appear to be a majority viewpoint, the minority position appears just often enough so that no definite concept can be forwarded for the labor practitioner's guidance.

The majority of decisions hold that even when a contract contains no general limitation on management's right to discharge, a just cause restriction is implied.[12]

One of the most respected arbitration authorities, Meyer S. Ryder, has said, "In the setting of labor contractual commitments and what they mean to benefit both employer and employee, to not have some reasonable and accepted justifiable basis for the disciplinary severance of an employment relationship is to mortgage the very stability in the workforce that the productive enterprise must want and have." [13]

Judge Norman N. Eiger, deciding a discharge dispute between Continental Airlines and the Teamsters, made this comment:

> Discharge is one of the most drastic measures a company can take against an employee. With his discharge comes loss of seniority rights, pay, and all the benefits secured by the employee under the collective bargaining Agreement.

> Although the instant Contract has no particular provision that an employee shall not be discharged without just cause, nevertheless, it is the considered opinion of the Arbitrator, in the light of overwhelming legal authority and precedent and in this day of enlightened labor-management relations, that such a provision is implicit and inherent in the Contract in question.

> To hold that a company can capriciously at its sole discretion without just cause discharge an employee would in effect nullify the provisions of the contract entered into by the parties.[14]

Arbitrators agreeing with this viewpoint will examine with extreme care an employer's claim that it has an unchallengeable right under the contract to discharge for any reason, just or unjust. Most arbiters find it difficult to conceive of a union's granting an employer totally unfettered authority. This does not mean that no labor agreements give the employer the unilateral right to discharge without need for cause, but such agreements are both few and unusual. As Arbitrator Saul Wallen has said, the meaning of the contract viewed as a whole "is that a limitation on the employer's right to discharge was created with the birth of the instrument. Both the necessity for maintaining the integrity of the contract's component parts and the very nature of collective bargaining agreements are the basis for this conclusion. . . ." [15] Although this comment was made during a hearing more than 20 years ago, it still carries force.

Where the contract is silent regarding any standard of cause or just cause, one arbitrator found that past practice demonstrated the parties' intentions to have some standard applied.[16]

Majority arbitral opinion holds that if a firm can use discharge to circumvent any right or benefit otherwise extended to employees under a contract, this reduces its commitment to a nullity. Most practitioners will agree that a company does not have this power unless contractual language establishes it beyond any doubt or question. But others have held that the absence of any express restriction in a contract on management's right to discharge shows an intention for this power to be unlimited. For example, Edgar L. Warren, in deciding a case involving Meletron Corp., expressed this view:

> While a discharge grievance can be presented, the Company is under no contractual obligation to justify the decision it has made.
>
> It is also the opinion of the Arbitrator that the security provisions of the Agreement do not modify the Company's right to discharge employees, with or without cause, without having its decision challenged in arbitration.[17]

THE BURDEN OF PROOF

One purpose of the labor agreement is to promote favorable relations between the company and its employees. This cannot be achieved if management acts under its contract without a fair and proper determination of the facts involved in any discipline or discharge action it takes. It must stand ready to support its allegations against employees charged with improper conduct. What this means in the submission of such an issue to arbitration is that the party bearing the burden of proof will be required to open the case and present its position first and will also be given the right to close the hearing with a position statement. Of course, this procedure may be altered or waived.

It seems to be a well-established tenet of labor relations that the burden of proof in disputes over discipline or discharge must be carried by the party holding the affirmative of the issue—that is, the party who initiated the challenged action. The employer is therefore called on to establish the facts it asserts as the basis for having taken positive corrective action.

Arbitrators differ on the quantity and quality of proof demanded from the employer. There are those who require that guilt be established "beyond reasonable doubt," as do our criminal courts. Labor arbitrators are inclined to impose this measurement when the charges are by nature criminal or involve substantial injury to the employee's work status, job security, or reputation.[18] Others see the burden of proof as carried if a "preponderance of the evidence" establishes a prima facie case. In such an instance, the burden of proof may actually transfer from one party to the other during the arbitration proceedings. An example will illustrate this.

Let us imagine that a firm has discharged an employee for incompetence. To prove the necessity for the disciplinary action, it presents evidence of poor-quality materials, bad parts, and a low productivity record. It establishes that the particular employee charged with the misconduct is in fact the offender, and it shows that the corrective action was appropriate to his act of misconduct and his record. This evidence constitutes a prima facie case. However, the union alleges that the poor work was not the product of the discharged employee and that his low productivity was the result of some factors beyond his control. At this point, the burden of proof transfers to the union; it cannot establish its claim merely by stating it, any more than the employer can, but must present evidence in support of the employee's innocence. If it does so, then the burden of proof transfers again, back to the employer.

Various arbitral opinions can be quoted to demonstrate the alternate requirements for supplying proper and adequate proof. Representative of one view is this comment by Arbitrator Harry H. Platt: "In a case of discharge, the burden of proof rests upon the Company to show, by a fair preponderance of the evidence, that the discharge of an employee was for good and sufficient cause." [19]

It is probably safe to say that most managements will argue for "a preponderance of the evidence" measurement. For example, a Steelworkers' arbitration bulletin reports a case at Great Lakes Steel Corporation decided by Arbitrator Louis A. Crane:

> Discharge for theft of Company property is upheld where the Board is convinced to a "confident certainty" that the Grievant committed the offense. Proof of guilt "beyond a reasonable doubt," as in a criminal prosecution, is not required. The Board is not concerned with enforcing the criminal law but with administering the collective bargaining agreement.[20]

On the other hand, some arbiters do adopt the standard of proof applied in criminal law. Arbitrator Robert J. Wagner put it this way: "In the discharge of two employees with over 13 and 12 years' service respectively, it would seem to be the responsibility of Management to show, beyond a reasonable doubt, that the employees are unable to perform a fair day's work." [21]

Arbitrator Mitchell M. Shipman, acting as the permanent arbitrator under the contract between the United Steelworkers and Bethlehem Steel, took the same approach in deciding a dispute over the discharge of employees for violating the no-strike clause:

> The evidence, at most, serves to develop a set of circumstances from which possible inferences might be drawn that the Complainants might have stopped other fellow employees from entering the plant. However, even if such inferences are available, they cannot suffice to sustain the Company's burden of proving beyond a reasonable doubt that the Complainants did stop or attempt to stop employees entering the plant. In light of the Complainants' unequivocal denial and disavowal of stopping employees from entering the plant, certainly something more than inferences must be required to sustain the Company's burden of proof. As much as [the Arbitrator] is mindful of the difficulties of proof, he must still look for sufficient substantial evidence that will leave no reasonable doubt that the Complainants are guilty as charged. [22]

Arbitrators are not in complete accord on the extent to which the rules of evidence and procedure applicable to criminal law should be considered in disputes over accusations of moral turpitude. However, a reading of the many cases involving such issues creates a definite impression that a majority of arbitrators require proof beyond a reasonable doubt.[23] An explanation of this philosophy was well articulated by Arbitrator James V. Altieri in settling a dispute between the Publishers Association of New York City and New York Stereotypers Union over the discharge of an employee for willful damage to company property:

> The Union cites a long array of awards holding that in cases of this kind the proof should be beyond a reasonable doubt. In the field of proper industrial relations, the philosophy is as valid as in other sociological and jurisprudential relationships, that it is better for an occasional guilty person to escape unpunished than to court the possibility, through less exacting norms, not only of punishing employees with loss of their jobs for acts of which they may not be guilty but [of placing] . . . upon them what might be an insurmountable burden in getting other employment. [24]

There is no question that an employee has certain clear responsibilities to his employer that are basic to their relationship. The reverse side of this coin is management's obligation not to discipline or discharge employees unless its expectations are reasonable and it has conducted an adequate and objective investigation to establish proof of the guilt of anyone accused of wrongdoing.

EVIDENCE

It would require a number of volumes to provide comprehensive treatment of the subject of evidence. This discussion will attempt rather to give a sample of the ways arbitrators commonly apply rules of evidence.

The strict legal rules of evidence and procedure prevailing in the courts are neither recommended nor practiced in the arbitration hearing, which is at most a quasi-judicial process. As was indicated in the preceding section, some arbiters are satisfied when a case is supported by a preponderance of the evidence. The majority seem to follow the criminal law requirement, particularly in discharge cases and more particularly where moral turpitude is alleged, that guilt be established beyond a reasonable doubt. What types of evidence meet these standards of proof?

The Quality of the Testimony

The wisest rule is always to use the best evidence available. For example, eyewitness accounts will certainly provide more compelling testimony than will hearsay. A check stub will be less persuasive evidence of a payment to an employee than a canceled check. A supervisor's testimony that an employee was not at work will be considered more conclusive if supported by payroll and production records and other such evidence resolving a question of disputed attendance. The reverse of this is also true: if only the supervisor's testimony is offered and documentary evidence is withheld, this failure to supply the best available evidence will probably reflect negatively on the company's claim.

The credibility of the witnesses weighs more heavily in the balance than their number. One should not be deluded into thinking that the more witnesses utilized to repeat a circumstance, the more credible the arbiter will find the information. As a matter of fact, it is quite possible for him to believe the party with fewer witnesses if their testimony seems sounder.[25] In this connection, it should also be remembered that the failure of a disciplined or discharged employee to take the stand in his own defense cannot be considered as evidence of guilt.

Circumstantial Evidence

Circumstantial evidence, which is frequently given in arbitration proceedings, is resorted to in the absence of any direct proof of the fact at issue. It consists in a number of peripheral events or conditions that, taken together, reasonably point to the fact.

An amusing case heard before the Federal Mediation and Conciliation Service illustrates one weakness of circumstantial evidence—its potential ambiguity. The case involved the discharge of a male factory employee for allegedly accosting a female office worker. It seems that the woman was walking down a 30-degree concrete ramp from one floor of the factory to another. The area was generally isolated, and no other employees appeared to be around. The woman reported to the personnel manager that as she walked down the ramp, she noticed the man in question approaching her, coming up. It later developed that she customarily walked past his machine and that they frequently exchanged pleasantries. She stated that as she was about to pass him on the ramp, he reached forward and placed his hands upon her chest. She then went to the personnel manager and demanded the man's discharge.

At the arbitration hearing, the man related a different version. He stated that as he came up the ramp, this fetching female appeared to catch her toe and fall toward him, and he merely raised his hands to catch her. He admitted that his hands had fallen on her chest, but this was purely fortuitous.

The conflicting testimony left the arbitrator uncertain and unsatisfied. He suggested that all parties convene at the plant and look at the situation for themselves.

As they stood gazing on the scene of the alleged misdeed, they saw a worker delivering materials on a dolly into the cavity under the ramp. After watching him come and go several times, the arbitrator decided to quiz him on the chance he might have information. This worker revealed that he was in and out of the cavity frequently throughout the day, and though he could see nothing that happened above him, he had heard an unusual sound on the day of the incident while he was working under the ramp: a female voice saying, "Ohhh!" He was uncertain whether it was an exclamation of alarm, pleasure, or relief. Because of this inconclusiveness, the discharged employee was reinstated with full back pay, full seniority, and virtue intact—at least, officially.

The opinion of the majority of arbitrators is that circumstantial evidence is real evidence, provided every other possible explanation that could controvert the company's arguments is eliminated. However, where too many imponderables remain, the doubt is resolved in the grievant's favor. Long experience has also taught the lesson that circumstantial evidence may in fact be more persuasive than direct evidence. But arbitrators understandably remain cautious. They know all too well of the "slip 'twixt the cup and the lip" in its use.

In deciding a dispute between the Illinois Bell Telephone Company and the IBEW, Meyer S. Ryder, one of the country's most highly regarded arbitrators, expressed how he felt about the burden of proof measurement to be used when circumstantial evidence is involved. He commented:

> The Chairman holds that in discharge matters where the employee offense being treated with carries along with it connotations of corruption and illegality, were the employee to be held guilty of the offense, the standard of evidentury proof to convict should be high. There should be no real subjective question of guilt in the minds of him or those who have to decide. Acceptable to this proposition should be evidence of circumstances or combination of circumstances such as leave no doubt that what is indicated is actually present. Should it be considered that the application of standards of proof in a criminal proceeding under the law go beyond and are greater than these standards, then the criminal law standards should not be held to apply in an industrial relations arbitration proceeding. Accordingly, the Chairman has applied the standards he has enunciated above to the discharge matters.[26]

Hearsay

Generally speaking, arbitrators reject hearsay evidence just as do judges in courts of law when it is properly objected to. The reason is fairly obvious—the contesting party has no chance to confront or cross-examine the declarant. Such testimony may be motivated by self-interest, malice, or spite; or it may be the product of an irresponsible person.

As has been stated before, arbitrators do not consider themselves bound by strict rules of evidence. The tendency in arbitration proceedings is to admit hearsay evidence and weigh it in light of the lack of opportunity to cross-examine. For example, Arbitrator Harold I. Elbert has ruled that doctors' certificates are admissible in an arbitration proceeding as proof of an employee's illness although they might be hearsay.[27] On this point, an examination of reported arbitration decisions indicates that medical certificates are commonly admitted in evidence and given weight by arbitrators in determining whether an employee was sick.[28]

Irrelevant Evidence

Arbitrators look askance at testimony or evidence introduced by the employer about events or circumstances that occur after a discharge action. In determining whether the action taken by the company fits the accusation against the employee, arbitrators are concerned only with his conduct preceding the discharge.

Arbitrator Harry J. Dworkin had to cope with this issue in a dispute involving the National Screw & Manufacturing Company and the UAW. The firm discharged an employee who, in violation of a plant rule, was absent for more than three days without having obtained approval. During the hearing, the employer introduced evidence that the grievant had been arrested for statutory rape before his dismissal and convicted of this crime after discharge. He had been absent from work because the police had advised him to remain at home during the investigation. Arbitrator Dworkin held that this did not excuse him from compliance with a plant rule requiring permission for absence and thus upheld the company's action. However, he made it clear that the employee's off-duty conduct for which he was arrested had no bearing, whether or not it would warrant disciplinary action in and of itself:

> The Grievant's subsequent conviction resulting from his plea of guilty could not be considered as providing a ground for discipline since the penalty was imposed prior to the indictment and conviction. At most, the subsequent conviction and particularly the admission of guilt at the trial could be considered as corroborative evidence bearing upon the Company's initial appraisal of the employee's conduct. It cannot, however, serve to retroactively provide justification for discipline in the absence of the just cause prior to the discharge.[29]

Equally irrelevant in discipline disputes is evidence of offers of compromise exchanged between the parties before instituting arbitration proceedings. Such evidence should be and usually is ruled inadmissible by arbitrators. This is so irrespective of whether the compromise offers were made orally or in writing. There are valid and obvious reasons for this. The primary purpose of the grievance procedure in the labor agreement is to provide the parties with machinery for resolving their differences without having to resort to arbitration. For this machinery to work effectively, the parties must both feel at liberty to exchange settlement offers freely. If their negotiations could later be used to the detriment of the party initiating them, the fundamental objective of the grievance procedure would be frustrated.

Lie Detectors

Employers seem to be using lie detectors increasingly, particularly in industrial discharge cases. For some time, an argument has been boiling in labor-management circles about the relevance of the polygraph test and its admissibility as evidence in arbitration hearings. Employers have been using its results as evidence of the guilt of discharged employees and referring to an employee's unwillingness to submit to the test as indicative of a desire to conceal guilt.

This controversy is probably an outgrowth of the dispute over the use of polygraph tests in criminal proceedings. *The Manual for Prosecuting Attorneys* states the reason the tests are not usually admitted in evidence by the courts: "Such tests have not yet gained such standing and scientific recommendation among physiological and psychological authorities as would justify the courts in admitting expert testimony deduced from the discovery, development and experiments thus far made." [30] Another authoritative source states:

> It would appear, at least in the absence of stipulation, that the courts almost uniformly reject the results of lie detector tests when offered in evidence for the purpose of establishing the guilt or innocence of one accused of a crime, whether the accused or the prosecution seeks its introduction. The reason most commonly assigned for the exclusion of such evidence is the contention that the lie detector has not as yet attained scientific acceptance as a reliable and accurate means of ascertaining truth or deception. [31]

A number of trial courts have allowed the testimony of lie detector examiners in instances where counsel for both sides had agreed to the test before it was given and stipulated that the examiner's interpretation could be used in evidence without objection from the party adversely affected by it. Presumably these conditions could make the tests admissible in arbitration proceedings as well.

The use of polygraph tests in arbitration proceedings has also received coverage in a well-written article by R. W. Fleming in the *Michigan Law Review*.[32] A reading of the published awards on this issue coupled with Dr. Fleming's article shows that arbitrators generally deny consideration of the results of lie detector examinations.

There seems to be little argument that the tests have substantial practical importance when they are conducted by competent and experienced people. Their greatest value would appear to derive from their psychological effect of inducing admissions from guilty persons. The majority of arbitrators nonetheless agree that the polygraph is not a reliable instrument for establishing the truth. At its current state of development, even its most ardent advocates do not claim that its accuracy is more that 75 percent. Arbitrators therefore tend to follow the courts on this issue.

Judge Norman N. Eiger ruled in an arbitration proceeding that he could not, in view of the majority position of the courts of the land, determine the rights of an individual according to the results of a lie detector test. He stated: "The Arbitrator holds [that] these tests . . . have no probative value and are not admissible as evidence in these proceedings." [33]

Arbitrator Albert A. Epstein commented somewhat more cautiously on the use of polygraph tests, but his decision was nonetheless the same:

> The use of the test has been the subject matter of much discussion in both court proceedings and arbitrations. There is no clear law or practice in this area. It is argued that there is always the possibility that the tests are not accurate and that the emotional state or condition of the individual being tested may affect the validity of the test. There is enough of a conflict among scientific authority and legal and arbitrative precedents to warrant a serious doubt about the probative value of the polygraph test. . . .[34]

Arbitrator James C. Vadakin was faced with an unusual situation in a case in which a company administered a lie detector test to its foreman as corroboration of his testimony on an altercation that an employee had had with him and that had led to the employee's discharge. The arbiter allowed the test results to be entered into the record of the hearing, but he accorded them no weight in reaching his decision.[35]

The closest one can come to an arbitral decision that accords with the use of lie detector tests is the finding in a case between Westinghouse Electric Corporation and the IUE. The employer had imposed disciplinary suspension on three wildcat strikers who were involved in assaulting a car containing another employee. During the processing of the grievances, both the grievants and their victim agreed to take polygraph tests, with the understanding that the results would be disclosed to the company and the union and be made available to any party for the purpose of resolving the grievance. At the arbitration hearing that followed, Arbitrator Al T. Singletary permitted the admission of the test results. Although he did not pass upon the reliability of the report of the polygraph examinations, he did observe that the conclusions reached in it were corroborated by the conclusions he drew from other evidence.[36]

The issue is perhaps best summed up in an article on the subject by Lee M. Burkey:

> Lie detector results, being incompetent evidence, cannot be made competent either by an employee's voluntary submission to it or by the fact that there are other circumstances indicating guilt. If there is no evidence of an employee's guilt other than lie detector results, sound principles of Anglo-American law would seem to require a presumption of innocence. Surely the sanctity of the individual and the protection of the innocent [justify] the rejection of the use of the polygraph even though a guilty few may profit thereby.
>
> . . . apparently the time has not come when the exercise of the highest intelligence and discretion of which the human mind is capable, that is, the ascertainment of truth, can be turned over to a machine. Science is still incomplete and truth is still illusive.[37]

Refusal to Take a Polygraph Test

What happens when an employee refuses to submit to a polygraph test? In a case involving Town and Country Food Company, Arbitrator Lewis found that a discharge for alleged insubordination was not justified on the basis of a refusal to take a lie detector test.[38]

Arbitrator William E. Simkin had to deal with the same problem. The Publishers Association of New York City contended that a grievant's refusal to submit to a lie detector test should be considered by the Tri-Partite Arbitration Board as supplemental evidence of his guilt. Simkin remarked:

> The Chairman supports the Union position that this feature of the case should be ignored by this Board. To put the matter bluntly, it is the

Chairman's position that this Board is required necessarily to judge the credibility of witnesses on the basis of their testimony and evidence submitted at the hearing and that no individual's refusal to submit to a lie detector test should prejudice him in any way.[39]

The following finding by Arbitrator Meyer S. Ryder is particularly significant on this question. In a refreshingly articulate decision resolving a dispute between the IBEW and the Illinois Bell Telephone Company, he expressed this well-reasoned view:

An innocent individual may lack confidence in his emotional stability whereby he may believe warrantedly or unwarrantedly that such a testing will show deception where there is none. Such an individual may refuse a testing as readily as may a guilty individual who desires to hide the truth. In many cases innocent individuals will confidently submit to such testing. Other innocent individuals may reluctantly submit because of the implicit social threat in their refusing in the setting of a plant community. It appears that the polygraph has been an effective instrument in indicating deception in the heavy preponderance of cases. However, where there is employee refusal to give consent to such testing, the refusal, standing by itself and coupled or not coupled with the presence of factual material giving reasonable suspicion of culpability, is not that kind of behavior that should be an offense in and of itself. To punish for refusing to consent on the basis that this is lack of cooperation appears to supply an overtone of being required to self-incriminate, a proposition repugnant to Anglo-Saxon legal codes.[40]

There is one exception to the general rule that refusal to take such tests is not incriminatory. That exception was expressed by Arbitrator Carroll R. Daugherty. Under a contract in which the union agreed that its plant guards would "cooperate fully" with the employer in the investigation of theft or other, similar security matters, the employer was held to have properly issued written warnings to guards for refusing to take a polygraph examination in connection with the theft of two television sets. By agreeing to "cooperate fully" in the contract, the union waived the employees' right to refuse to submit to polygraph tests.[41]

Chapter 3

The Appropriateness
of the Penalty

To circumscribe the ground that this chapter will cover, let us define first what it will not. It will not discuss the harshness or severity of penalties as they are imposed. It will not dwell on how well or how poorly the punishment fit the crime. It will refer only in passing to the guidelines that arbitrators follow in substituting their own judgment for management's where the action taken did not contravene an explicit contractual provision. These questions are dealt with in other parts of the book.

Chapter 2 has already thrown some light on these issues, citing in particular Arbitrator Carroll R. Daugherty's renowned seven criteria for deciding discipline cases. It has also introduced the view of a number of other practitioners that arbitrators should accept management's judgment, if they deem it fair, when the agreement gives the company the right to discipline.[1] The majority appear to do so where reasonable criteria are applied, as we have seen, though an American Arbitration Association study of 321 discharge cases occurring within one year found that one out of every three resulted in a divided award, generally reinstatement without back pay.[2]

Where discipline other than discharge was involved, management's original decision was upheld more often, but divided awards were still found in 10 percent of the cases.[3] In mitigating a penalty, arbitrators generally reason that the discipline imposed was not reasonable in view of the worker's past record or of the company's past practice in promulgating and enforcing the rule.

With these topics enlarged on elsewhere, the discussion that follows will attempt to treat a number of questions. Seven major issues will be covered, among others:

1. Is demotion ever an appropriate penalty, and if so, when and under what circumstances?
2. When is a quit a quit, and when is it considered a constructive discharge?
3. How recent and how similar to a current offense should past misconduct be to have a bearing on a disciplinary case?
4. Can a discipline or discharge penalty that in itself is merited become inappropriate because it is imposed too soon or too long after the offense? How short a period makes it precipitous, and how much time lapse makes it stale?
5. Should an employee ever be disciplined twice for a single violation of a rule? What is double jeopardy, and when is a sanction against it applied by arbitrators as a bar to management's action?
6. Is it proper to impose a suspension whose terminal point is either indefinite or contingent on an employee's apology or compliance with a given order?
7. What impact does a procedural defect, such as failure to give written notice of an impending disciplinary action, have on a case at arbitration?

When one is contemplating these questions, it is important to remember that an arbitration decision is in no sense a final and binding ruling on a particular issue. The justification for this condition, as we have seen, is that each case must turn on the language of the contract involved. Despite this, rulings in other cases often have persuasive value with arbiters because they provide guidance on how practitioners generally evaluate similar or comparable disputes.

DEMOTION

Demotion can take a form other than a reduction in position or rate of pay. A worker may very well consider that he has been demoted if he is transferred from a desirable shift to a less desirable one. At least this was the opinion of two senior employees at Parkside Manor, a nursing home, who were advised less than an hour before the end of their workday of their transfer from day to night duty. The contract under which they functioned, which was held by the Building Service

Employees Union, contained provisions enabling employees to choose their shift on the basis of seniority.

The background of this dispute contains facts that were clearly established at the hearing held before Arbitrator A. Lee Belcher.[4] Their conduct included refusal to take instructions and carry out orders, failure to give proper care to patients, inordinate amounts of time spent having coffee in the utility room, frequent delays in answering the patients' call bells, and loud arguments in hallways, to the embarrassment of management. In apparent frustration over such behavior, management unilaterally decided to transfer the two erring employees to a night shift, assuming, as it indicated in the arbitration hearing, that the grievants would prefer this alternative to termination of employment. However, its choice was one that clearly violated the terms of the agreement, and as Clair V. Duff stated in a case he decided for the General Telephone Company of Pennsylvania, "The principle of labor-management relations is that denial of a contract benefit is not an appropriate form of discipline." [5]

Although the employer's evidence and testimony regarding the behavior of the two workers were fully persuasive, Arbitrator Belcher ruled that to sustain management's position would be to deny seniority rights granted the employees by contract. In other words, the company's action constituted an inappropriate penalty under the contract despite the employees' proven misconduct.

Demotion or Discipline?

A small majority of arbitrators frown on demotion as a form of discipline in the absence of a specific contractual provision authorizing such a penalty. The contrary view, held by a good many labor relations practitioners, is that management has retained its right to use demotion for disciplinary purposes unless the agreement expressly limits its right to do so. The school of thought that calls demotion an improper penalty seems more correct, and cases will be supplied to substantiate this opinion.

The reasons behind this viewpoint are numerous and varied. By demoting an employee, management can be imposing a penalty of indefinite duration. Its action can affect the seniority rights of not only the penalized worker but also others, who then become unintended victims. It can weaken the demoted employee's job security by making him more vulnerable to layoff. It may jeopardize his ability to obtain more meaningful and profitable positions in the future. It is too often a substitute for intestinal fortitude—an easy or at least less troublesome way out of a situation meriting discharge or another form of discipline. Further, it can result in the imposition of unequal penalties: one worker can be demoted three labor grades while another who is guilty of the same offense under similar circumstances may be demoted two or four. In essence, demotion should be related to the employee's competence and qualifications for the job, not to breaches of plant rules, which call for discipline.

Moreover, if an employee has the ability to perform a job and is withholding it, this constitutes a condition that is subject to correction through progressive discipline. The reason for the behavior is really irrelevant. Whether it arises from a misplaced sense of independence, work group pressures, or circumstances in his private life, there is no justification for it as long as any such conditions are within his control.

A case involving the Bethlehem Steel Company embodies this view. The arbiter held that management's demotion of an employee was improper because his record indicated that he had the requisite ability for the job, stating that disciplinary action rather than demotion was the proper remedy where substandard performance was found to be temporary.[6] The two significant facts are that the employee possessed ability and that he had demonstrated it. His failure to apply it to his task was merely temporary. The expectation was that he would regain his previous level of performance.

The arbiter of another dispute held that the Boeing Company could use demotion when the employee was not capable of performing the work, but it was not entitled to demote where the evidence showed that errors were the result of negligence rather than inability.[7] Similarly, an arbitrator deciding a case involving the Republic Steel Corporation ruled that it could not use demotion as a form of discipline for occasional carelessness or failure to obey instructions on the job.[8]

All these decisions express the concept that as long as an employee is able and qualified to carry out his work, his failure to do so represents a fault that should be corrected by discipline rather than demotion.

The Testing Period for Competence

How long must an employee remain on a job before he should be considered qualified for it? In a case between Du Pont and the Textile Workers Union, almost five years was not long enough. The arbitrator sanctioned management's demotion of a worker for incompetence 4½ years after his promotion to the job. In the arbiter's opinion, the mere fact that this employee had been retained in the position for such a period did not warrant a finding that he was qualified for it.[9] This decision endorsed the concept that management possesses the right to demote in the absence of contractual provisions to the contrary.

Arbitrator Clair V. Duff upheld management's demotion of a floor inspector who had five years' tenure after several verbal and two written warnings to him for his failure to reject products with visible defects. This employee was the only inspector on the particular job and had an important role in determining the quality of the final product. The decision contains an elaboration on the standard theme. Duff concluded that the demotion was imposed not for disciplinary or discriminatory reasons but rather because management wanted to improve quality standards in the plant.[10] A somewhat similar case reaching the same conclusion occurred at the Machine Products Company.[11] However, demotions like these—for carelessness or negligence —have been upheld because of the connection the deficiency has with job qualifications.[12]

Arbitrators may restrict management's right to demote even where an employee's capabilities are in question if it exercises its power in an arbitrary or capricious manner, thus jeopardizing job security guarantees that employees derive from seniority provisions.[13]

QUITS VERSUS DISCHARGES

The time-tested proverb that actions speak louder than words applies as one of the principles operating in cases where the employee is charged with having quit his job but argues that he didn't.

The Essential Ingredient: Intent

The question of whether an employee's action constitutes a quit is one that arbitrators have often explored and discussed. Typical of the majority viewpoint on this score is the opinion expressed by Whitley P. McCoy in a case involving LaFollette Shirt Company:

> Unless some clauses of the contract specifically spell out what shall constitute a quit, the matter is one of intent accompanied by an act. The mere going home, leaving the job, is not a quit unless it can be seen that the employee intended a permanent quitting. It might be insubordination, and ground for discharge, but it would not be a resignation unless the employee so intended.[14]

Arbitrator James F. Bell has put it equally well: "[To quit,] the employee must manifest by words or action an intent to terminate and finally abandon his employment accompanied by an overt act carrying out the intent; the element of finality is indispensable as is the one of intent." [15]

The essential features of a discharge are that management takes positive action and communicates it to the employee in words clearly stating its intention to sever the work relationship completely. A quit or resignation has basically the same features: the employee must take some positive step, dispassionately and willfully and not under duress, and must notify the company in terms that indicate his intention to terminate his employment permanently.

The problem with most disputes over whether a worker has quit or been discharged is that the situations usually arise out of anger or excitement—the passion of the moment. The employee's conduct is often not governed by cool reason, and he vents his feelings spontaneously in thoughtless remarks.

This was the case in a dispute decided by Arbitrator Israel Ben Scheiber, one of the statesmen of the arbitral community. During a heated discussion about being laid off for lack of work, an employee said he intended to quit. However, in less than an hour he came back, accompanied by two union officials, and made it abundantly clear that he was not actually quitting. Also significant was the fact that he did not turn in his key and plate wrench, as was customary when an employee quit, although his supervisor requested him to do so. These two actions, one positive and one negative, were plainly not those of a man intending to leave his job. An examination of some of Arbitrator Scheiber's reflections on this and other such disputes is enlightening:

We deal here with an employee who has invested 7½ years of his life with this Company and, during that time, appears to have rendered service which was at least sufficiently satisfactory to have enabled him to retain his job during that period. This fact, and the seniority provisions, pension rights, paid holidays and other important benefits which had accrued to the employee, entitled him to have his right to his job carefully balanced against the results of heated and hasty actions. . . .

Situations and actions and especially words spoken while the parties are in a state of tension and so emotionally involved as to be incapable of calm, cool and rational thinking, and coupled too with their inability to realize the seriousness of the words spoken in the heat and excitement of the moment, are by no means unusual in the uneasy coexistence which, in general, marks the relationship of Labor and Management. Therefore, there is a clear tendency on the part of Arbitrators, in the interests of both parties, to make reasonable allowances, therefore, where facts exist which justify such action. . . .

On these facts and on this record, to sustain the contention of the Company that, under the circumstances of this case, the Grievant was a "voluntary quit" would bring about an excessively harsh and unreasonable result in situations like the present, situations which an examination of some of the scores of the reported "voluntary quit" cases shows to be by no means unusual.[16]

The absence of an overt act exhibiting intention to quit is a meaningful circumstance. The lengths to which this premise may be taken was clearly shown in a case where an employee was off on a medical leave of absence and for a period of 80 days let inquiries from the company go unanswered. When he finally did attempt to return to work, management advised him that it considered him a quit, although he had not previously, nor did he then, manifest any interest in permanently discontinuing his employment relationship. The arbiter held that if the company had expressed dissatisfaction with his excuse, it could have discharged him, and such action "would have been difficult to overturn." But this was not the case. The employer's action was premised not on absenteeism but on the claim of a voluntary quit. Thus concluding, the arbiter held the grievance to have merit and upheld it.[17]

The same result has been reached in a variety of other cases.[18] A contrary decision is found in a number of disputes, but each contains evidence of some calm and deliberate action on the part of the employee, such as going to the personnel office and demanding his pay, taking his own tools home with him, or giving notice.[19]

Evidence of this kind was established in a dispute between Stewart-Warner Corporation and the United Steelworkers.[20] The question before Arbitrator Theodore K. High was whether a severance constituted a "voluntary quit" or a "constructive discharge." Management claimed the former term applied; the union, of course, contended the latter did. The answer to this question would either involve the company in or exempt it from proving just cause for the job termination.

The facts of the case were these. In the course of a shift of work, a female employee had an argument with a married male employee with whom she had developed a romantic liaison. After the argument, her supervisor advised her that such problems were disruptive to work and could lead to her friend's losing his job. She then had a discussion with her friend and emerged from it highly upset. Following this, she did three things evidencing the intent that arbiters consider as an essential element of quitting. First, before leaving the plant, she went to her boss and handed him her hat and safety glasses. Normal plant procedure was for her to place them in her locker. Second, she did not dispute the company's withholding her final paycheck in satisfaction of an outstanding loan with it. Third, she did not report for work for a few days following her departure from the plant.

This was clearly a "voluntary quit" and not a "constructive discharge," and so the arbiter ruled. She was not provoked by management to follow the course she chose. Had she been, the entire complexion of the case might have been affected. Her three actions did not demonstrate intent to return to work. Had she placed her hat and glasses in her own locker, protested the withholding of her check, or even reported for work on the following day, she might have explained her behavior as solely the product of anger and not a desire to discontinue the employment relationship. But when all that did happen was put together, the situation clearly fit the definition of a quit.

Contractual Definitions

In the remarks of Arbitrator Whitley P. McCoy quoted earlier, he mentioned that certain clauses in a labor agreement might spell out what constitutes a quit. Such was the situation in a dispute between Red Wing, Minn., and the Boot and Shoe Workers Union. This agreement provided that an employee who walked off his job during working hours without permission from the appropriate supervisor would be deemed to have terminated his employment. An employee insisted on leaving work to go fishing although her foreman denied her permission to do so, whereupon the company considered her to have voluntarily terminated her employment. The union protested that the company had unreasonably refused her permission to take the day off, that her absence had not created a crucial manpower shortage, and that termination was too severe an action, a warning being sufficient. However, the factor most determining with Arbiter Daniel G. Jacobowski was the controlling language of the contract, which called this a termination initiated by the employee.[21]

Arbitrator Joseph Shister encountered a rare situation in a case between U.S. Corrugated-Fibre Box Company of Alabama and the United Mine Workers of America, District 50. In this dispute, the company initially discharged an employee. It then reduced this penalty to a one-week suspension without attaching any conditions regarding the employee's right to file a grievance. However, the employee adamantly refused to return to work until the company rescinded the disciplinary layoff. He just stayed away. The question this raised was whether he should be considered a discharge or a quit. The answer is both yes and no. Yes, the company initially discharged him. But after reducing this to a lesser penalty, did it in effect discharge him again, upon his failure to report for work within three consecutive days as contractually provided? No, he was not discharged on this second occasion; he quit voluntarily through his own act of absenting himself for a period longer than his contract privileges allowed.[22]

Induced Quits

How do labor practitioners rule when a quit, even one that breaches a contractual provision, has been induced by an employer or perhaps even forced by some coercive or discriminatory act? There have been cases where a company has imposed conditions on an employee that are not related to his job or work performance and that have caused him to resign. What may seem a resignation may in fact turn out to be a forced quit, particularly if the company's reasons for applying its conditions are motivated by discrimination.

The National Labor Relations Board has ruled in many cases that an employer's action showed unlawful discrimination and thus equaled a forced quit or constructive discharge. For example, workers who quit Monroe Auto Equipment Co. after being transferred to more disagreeable jobs or work assignments were considered by the Board to have been constructively discharged.[23] It was not a quit when three employees walked off their jobs on the day that a union won an NLRB election. The Board considered it significant that the company removed its heaters from the plant just before the workers left.[24]

Nor was the resignation of an employee voluntary when he agreed to quit after a company official offered him a recommendation for a job somewhere else provided he first sign a resignation card. He was then threatened with having his pay withheld unless he signed it.[25] In another case, a union representative ordered an employee off his job with the company's permission, telling him in fact that unless he left voluntarily, he would get thrown out. Judging discretion the better part of valor, the employee elected to leave. The Board could not agree that he had resigned.[26]

Rulings similar to these of the National Labor Relations Board are typical when such disputes are resolved in arbitration hearings. The

concept behind such findings represents the viewpoint of the overwhelming majority of professional arbiters. Let us review a few
examples.

A worker at one firm was informed that his work as a class A com-
positor in the company printing shop was unsatisfactory for a variety
of reasons, and he was told to choose between tendering a resignation
or being discharged. After some hesitation, the grievant stated that
he would resign. When the dispute was heard before Arbitrator Daniel
J. Dykstra, one of the questions to be resolved was whether the grievant
resigned or was discharged. The arbiter's remarks in this connection
are a clear and lucid expression of what most of his colleagues would
say:

> The Grievant on December 28 was confronted with a Hobson's choice,
> resign or be told your services are terminated. Under such circumstances,
> it cannot seriously be argued that his action was a voluntary one. He had
> no real freedom of choice. Surely, if it is concluded that a discharge
> under the circumstances alleged was improper, it would be incongruous
> to hold that such impropriety could not be challenged because the em-
> ployee was forced into tendering a resignation. For this reason, it is con-
> cluded that the Company's action amounted to a discharge.[27]

The late Donald A. Crawford decided an unusual case on this point.
An employee was discharged for theft. During a meeting between
management and union representatives, he was given the opportunity to
resign instead of being discharged. If he did so, he would be eligible
to receive some $400 in vacation pay. If he did not, he would lose this
money as a discharged employee. The company also took the position
that resignation would preclude the employee's filing any grievance.
But after this meeting and after quitting, he did so. In the hearing, the
arbiter could not find that the worker had quit voluntarily, given the
situation he found himself faced with. He had already been discharged. Had he not quit, he would have remained discharged. He
therefore had no alternative but to quit.[28]

Withdrawing a Resignation

Another issue that has plagued arbitrators, unions, and employers
alike might be phrased, can an employee who quit unquit? In other
words, if an employee quits by an overt and willful act, has he the
privilege or indeed the right to change his mind? If so, up to what
point may he exercise it and at what point does he sacrifice it?

The question of whether an employee who resigns has a right to rescind that decision is not easily answered. Perhaps this is because there is no preponderant arbitral viewpoint on this issue. Two examples will illustrate the divergent holdings.

On September 23, a worker notified his foreman that he wanted to quit as of October 4. On October 1, the employee learned that the new job was no longer available, and sought to revoke his decision to quit. The company refused to recognize the attempted rescission, however, taking the position that he had effectively terminated his employment by submitting his resignation and that his attempt to withdraw his notice did not restore him to the status of an employee. The contract contained no provision specifically governing resignation and attempted rescission though it did state that an employee was divested of seniority rights when he quit voluntarily or was discharged for just cause.

Arbitrator Harry J. Dworkin ruled that the company did not act improperly, for he deemed that the employee had quit his job voluntarily and therefore his decision could be rescinded only through mutual agreement. The arbiter viewed this case as a matter of a simple and deliberate resignation that permanently severed the relationship between the employer and the employee.[29]

An example of an opinion contrary to Arbiter Dworkin's is found in a case involving the Consumers Union of the United States Inc. The arbitrator held that an employee might withdraw his resignation before its effective date because the company had not changed its own position on the basis of the employee's "declaration." [30] One of the principal factors that may influence an arbitrator's conclusions in this regard is the lengths to which management has gone in acting upon a received resignation. That is, he will give consideration to whether the employee's resignation withdrawal will cause the company administrative inconvenience or additional costs. Has it committed itself to a replacement for the departing employee? Has it already brought a replacement onto the payroll? Has it arranged employee transfers to accommodate the job vacuum? If so, arbitrators seem less inclined to permit resignation withdrawals. On the other hand, if the rescission will cause the employer little or no inconvenience, arbitrators appear to favor allowing the withdrawal of the resignation.

THE APPLICABILITY OF PAST OFFENSES

When considering what penalty to impose in a case, how far back can management reasonably go in reviewing the employee's work record? Moreover, can it properly take into account previous offenses that differ in kind from the infraction he is currently charged with? Unions often argue that reference to a worker's disciplinary record subjects him to double jeopardy, as we will see later in this chapter. Occasionally the labor agreement provides an arbitrator with some guidance on these questions.

The Recency of Earlier Offenses

An employee received discipline on April 29 and again on September 10. He was given a two- and a six-day suspension on the two occasions respectively. On October 29 of the same year, he was discharged after he left his work station without permission for the purpose of requesting a conference with a foreman concerning another employee's grievance. He did this in his capacity as departmental steward. The union objected to the introduction of the grievant's two previous disciplines into evidence. The comments of the arbitrator in this connection are relevant and telling:

> This Arbitrator overruled the Union counsel's objections regarding the acceptance and consideration of evidence of such prior discipline. It was explained at that time that such evidence was relevant and material to the question of whether or not the penalty of discharge was excessive. Arbitrators generally allow the introduction of evidence of proper discipline for such purpose, providing the same is not too remote. It is manifest that the parties contemplated that prior discipline would be considered with regard to whether the penalty of discharge would be too severe. It is expressly stated in Sec. 7, Para. C., Subpara. 2, that disciplinary steps placed in writing will be void after two years from date of issuance. If, as claimed by the Union, this Arbitrator has no authority to consider such prior discipline, then it is inconceivable why such language should be placed in the Agreement. The two incidents of prior discipline each occurred within two years of the date of the discharge; in fact, they both occurred within the same year as the discharge.

> It is the finding of this Arbitrator that the discipline imposed was in accordance with the progressive disciplinary plan provided for in Sec. 7 of the Agreement.[31]

The same reasoning brought a contrary finding in a dispute between United States Steel Corporation and the United Steelworkers. The grievant was protesting two separate disciplinary suspensions for alleged failure to perform his job duties. A contractual provision prohibited the use in arbitration hearings of any records of disciplinary actions that had occurred five or more years before an event under examination. The company nonetheless introduced a reprimand form at the hearing and in its brief showing that the grievant had been disciplined more than five years earlier. Although the company contended that it had not relied on the prior disciplinary incident, the very nature of the form made it a necessary and important part of the evidence in the present case. If in fact it was so irrelevant, why was it referred to at all? The contractual statute of limitations on the previous discipline had expired. "Therefore," the arbiter ruled, "solely because of the improper use of past disciplinary action in the instant arbitration proceeding the grievances must be sustained." [32]

The basic concept behind this decision is sound. Discipline should be corrective and rehabilitative, not punitive. Management's objective in resorting to it should be to correct improper behavior where possible. The penalty imposed should be just harsh enough to produce change, no harsher. Moreover, if the company really intends for discipline to be corrective rather than punitive, it should assume that the majority of employees involved will respond affirmatively. Therefore, when an employee has presented no recurring problems and violated no rules after a reasonable time has passed, he should be regarded as rehabilitated. Offenses after this time should not be evaluated in the shadow of old incidents that have grown stale and inapplicable.

What constitutes a reasonable period after which previous offenses will no longer be considered is a factor that is decided within each bargaining relationship. In the U.S. Steel case just described, a contractual period of five years constituted the statute of limitations. Other labor-management groups agree to one or two years. Sometimes the period is contractually defined; in other instances, the employer simply advises supervisors of a general yardstick to follow consistently.

The Similarity of Earlier Offenses

The critical question may arise in an arbitration hearing of whether prior disciplines should be taken into account if they were imposed for a different kind of offense. For example, a supervisor told a worker twice in one day not to pile trash outside the incinerator so close to the hot ashes as to catch fire and burn. The order was disregarded both times. The next day, which was May 6, 1966, the supervisor reviewed the worker's disciplinary record for the previous two years. It revealed the following incidents and led to the man's discharge:

February 5 [1965]. Four-day disciplinary layoff for reporting production in excess of actual amount of work done in connection with incentive pay.

February 11. Written reprimand for operating scrap truck in walking aisle, causing an accident.

February 20. Discharged for falsification of work records in connection with incentive pay. This discharge was rescinded on March 8, which resulted in a disciplinary layoff of seventeen days.

November 3. Written reprimand for two accidents while driving Company automobile, both of which caused damage to the automobile.

March 31 [1966]. Oral reprimand for excessive absenteeism.[33]

The union lodged a grievance protesting the consideration of the employee's entire disciplinary record for two reasons: it was stale, and the prior offenses were not related to the most recent offense since none was for insubordination. The arbiter disagreed:

The Union very earnestly and vigorously contended that the Company did not have the right to review the entire disciplinary record of the Grievant for the prior two years but was limited to considering only disciplinary action for like offenses. . . . Under this proposition the two disciplinary layoffs for falsifying records could only be considered in connection with a further charge of improperly stating production on his incentive report. If the Grievant had another automobile accident within two years then the Company could review the written reprimand concerning the two prior accidents but only this reprimand. The position of the Union is understandable as it is presenting the best possible case it can for the Grievant. The review of disciplinary records is set forth in Section 6 of Article I, which provides as follows:

"Disciplinary records may be used as a basis for further disciplinary action for a period up to two years."

The above provision is very clear and explicit. . . . It does not restrict the review to disciplinary records "of like offenses" as the Union urges. . . . Accordingly, the Company had the right to review the entire disciplinary record for the prior two years and is not limited to disciplinary action for insubordination.[34]

In sum, the arbiter ruled that the earlier offenses, diverse though they were even in themselves, added enough weight to the employee's misconduct of May 5 to justify his discharge.

At the Wheland Products Div. of Gordon Street Inc., a new contract was negotiated with a provision stipulating that "In case of infraction of the Company rules, the Company will follow an operating policy of progressive disciplinary action (verbal warning, written reprimand, layoff, termination), except in extenuating circumstances." [35]

Under this contractual language, the employer imposed a three-day disciplinary suspension on a crane operator for his third offense—falling asleep in his cab while his crane was holding a heavy load of steel beams suspended above the plant floor. The union objected. It argued that the layoff was too severe, first because the offense was minor and second because the contractual procedure for administering discipline had not been followed, and that the requisite verbal warning and written reprimand must have been given within the preceding year or at least the term of the current contract. The arbitrator dealt with this contention as follows:

> In the instant case the Arbitrator cannot find from the evidence that there has been a practice mutually agreed to and followed wherein disciplinary actions are disregarded after one year. In view of the Grievant's past disciplinary record and of the nature of the offense in question, the Arbitrator must find that "just cause" existed for the imposition of the three-day layoff.
>
> Such past record would also satisfy the policy of progressive disciplinary action prescribed by the last paragraph of Section 2 of Article II if it were applicable. Although this provision is new with the present Contract, no intent therein appears to erase a disciplinary record accumulated prior to the beginning date of the current Agreement. The aim of progressive discipline is to treat the first offender more leniently than the repeater. The latter has normally indicated by his past record that he requires more severe measures to bring him into compliance with the accepted standards of employee behavior and performance. This objective would not be served by wiping an employee's past record clean when a new contract is signed. In the absence of express language in the Agreement to this effect, the Arbitrator cannot infer such an intent.[36]

On the issue of the severity of disciplinary action, a grievant's behavior record is relevant unless the contract provides that incidents before a certain date are to be disregarded. Except where the extreme penalty of discharge is imposed, the principal purpose of corrective discipline is to lead the employee back to an appropriate level of conduct. For this reason, arbitrators may regard any previous offenses, whatever their nature, as applicable to a current rule infraction.

THE TIMING OF THE DISCIPLINARY ACTION

This question divides into two issues. One deals with how quickly management may impose a penalty on an employee following a rule violation. The second involves what constitutes an unreasonably long time lapse between offense and discipline.

Rapid Imposition

How short can the time span be between a violation and the penalty for it? How about 15 minutes? This was the exceptional question raised in a grievance lodged against the S. D. Warren Company by the United Paper Makers and Paper Workers.

One afternoon an employee was ordered by his supervisor to move some material. He refused to do so on the basis that it was not within his job classification. The supervisor then issued a warning slip. In the arbitration hearing, the parties were not in complete agreement as to what occurred from that point onward. It appears that the worker sought out his union representatives for advice. When the supervisor returned to the work area 15 minutes later, he observed that the task had still not been done. He again approached the grievant and ordered him to move the material. Whether or not the employee actually refused once more was in dispute between the parties. It seems clear, however, that he told the foreman the union representatives would come in a few minutes and he wanted their help in discussing the problem. The foreman thereupon issued a seven-day disciplinary layoff for what he considered a second offense.

At the hearing, the company contended that the grievant had refused to obey a work order on two occasions; thus there were two separate offenses and two penalties were justified. It argued further that no time interval was necessary between the first and second steps of the disciplinary procedure. The union raised three points. First, the task was not within the grievant's job classification. Therefore, he had no duty to perform it. Second, even if the warning issued were deemed proper, the disciplinary layoff should not be, for the issuance of this penalty denied the employee an opportunity to file and process his grievance. Third, when the worker was directed to perform the task the second time, he did not refuse to do so but instead requested implementation of the grievance machinery.

Fortunately for the parties, the dispute was heard before one of the most astute members of the profession, Meyer S. Ryder.

On the first of the union's arguments, he ruled that the employee was obligated to accept the assignment and then file a grievance. With regard to the propriety of the company's administering two disciplinary penalties within 15 minutes, the arbitrator stated as follows:

The Arbitrator agrees with the Company that once the first step of the disciplinary procedure is completed, the Company does not have to wait until the issue is settled to move to the second step. But it is also clear that once a warning has been issued, the employee has the right to seek advice from his Union representative, file a grievance, and seek disposition of the matter. This the Grievant was attempting to do. His seeking of advice and help was in regard to the propriety of the order to do the work, which can be questioned under the warning which followed his refusal to do the work as ordered. He was clearly following proper procedure in this regard and it would appear to be the duty of the Foreman to hear the grievance. If, after such a hearing, the Foreman denied the grievance and ordered the Grievant to do the job, it would clearly be the obligation of the Grievant to perform [the work] while carrying the grievance to the next step of the grievance procedure. If the Grievant again refused, the Foreman would be within his rights in moving to the second step of the disciplinary procedure.

In view of the foregoing, it is clear that the Grievant was acting within his rights in asking to have the grievance heard. For this reason, the Arbitrator must hold that the Foreman, in proceeding so quickly, denied the Grievant that right; thus, the issuance of the seven-day layoff penalty was not in order at the time it was issued.[37]

Delayed Imposition

How soon after an offense should punishment be applied? The general answer is that management may delay imposing a penalty for a reasonable time but should have sufficient justification for the postponement. Arbitrators sometimes find that excessive delay resembles double jeopardy. They reason that the threat of punishment hanging over the employee's head, perhaps for months, constitutes punishment in and of itself, so that when the ax finally falls he experiences a second punishment for the same crime.

This was the view of the arbitrator deciding a dispute between Ashland Oil, Inc. and the Oil, Chemical and Atomic Workers Union. Although management was found to have a right to impose a five-day suspension on a worker for sleeping on the job, it damaged its cause by postponing enforcement of the penalty. The arbiter's conclusions exemplify how this issue is often decided:

Had the Company enforced the imposition of the five-day layoff when Mr. Bright returned from his vacation on August 15, or shortly thereafter, there would have been no question concerning the propriety of its action. The remaining question for consideration is the right of the Company to postpone, for its own convenience, the imposition of the five-day disciplinary layoff from August 15 to December 26. This was a period of over four months during which the employee had hanging over him the threat of a layoff without knowing whether or when it would be enforced. In fact, he believed that no further action would be taken as he had been so informed by his Foreman. During this interim he took seriously the advice given him by the Superintendent to avoid drowsiness and not only helped himself but also helped others. He apparently conducted himself properly and satisfactorily performed his duties in this period of time.

While postponing of the imposition of disciplinary action does not amount to double jeopardy, it does have some of the elements thereof. Holding the threat of the penalty over the employee for approximately four months is something of a penalty in itself. Double penalties for the same offense are contrary to our concept of justice and fairness. There is no principle in law under which the State can postpone, for its own convenience, the imposition of an announced penalty.[38]

A divergent point of view was strongly put forward by another arbitrator. A one-week suspension was scheduled to be imposed on an employee in accordance with contractual disciplinary procedures for excessive absenteeism. The employer postponed the suspension for 10 weeks, and as a result, a grievance was filed. In the arbitration hearing, the union argued that the delay subjected the grievant to double jeopardy and that she should be paid for the time lost because she had been intimidated and led to believe a penalty would not be exacted. The opinion drafted by Arbitrator George E. Strong includes the following comments, which indicate his outlook on such an issue:

The postponement of a disciplinary penalty is not double jeopardy. There has been no attempt to retry or punish her twice for her third offense of excessive absenteeism.

. . . the knowledge that a mandatory penalty will occur within a reasonable but uncertain time could assist in correcting excessive absenteeism, much as probation may influence offenders toward reform. The purpose of industrial discipline is corrective and not punitive so some other rationale than double jeopardy should be used if penalties are to be imposed on an employer for any unreasonable procedural delays. . . .[39]

A postponement of a suspension at the Geneva Steel Company was likewise upheld. An employee absented himself for three working days to go deer hunting without either asking for or receiving permission. Some days after his return, he was advised that he was to be suspended from work without pay for four working days as a penalty. This was confirmed in a written notification that also specified the dates of the suspension as November 15–17 and 20. Later these dates were changed to November 20–23. A grievance was filed, the union maintaining that the company had acted improperly in postponing the penalty period to more than 30 days after the offense.

Commenting on the delay, Arbitrator Ralph T. Seward made these observations:

> As to the postponement of the Grievant's actual suspension, the Company explained that during the last days in October and the first weeks in November, a maximum number of maintenance men were needed in the Rolling Mills. The Grievant's suspension was made effective as soon as efficient operations permitted. The postponement did not require C_____ to work during the interim under an indefinite threat of punishment since he was notified of his suspension less than a week after his offense, and since neither the nature [nor the] duration of the penalty was thereafter changed.[40]

This case contains several elements that merit emphasizing. No double jeopardy was involved here. The worker knew what would happen and when. The employer had a valid reason for delaying the suspension; although one might cast a dubious eye on a delay elected by management to accommodate its administrative convenience, there was sound business justification in this case, with no evidence of discrimination. Also, the penalty was imposed at the earliest convenient time. These were surely all factors that weighed in the employer's favor.

DOUBLE JEOPARDY

It is a well-established principle in labor-management relations that an employee cannot be punished twice for one offense. This is evidently an outgrowth of our constitutional prohibition against subjecting a person in a criminal proceeding to double jeopardy. The basis for the legal rule is the view that to try and then retry an accused for the same act would be an oppressive exercise of the power of the state against the individual. Our notions of fairness are offended by the thought.

This rule has been considered to have applicability to disciplinary proceedings in an industrial plant,[41] for, as one commentator has said, double penalties "would be contrary to fundamental concepts of justice." [42]   Consequently, an employee is entitled to regard a single punishment as final for a particular misconduct. [43]

There have been many hearings in which a union has argued double jeopardy in its defense of a member. A number of them were examined in the previous section. Reviewing several others will help determine what falls within and what outside the framework of this concept.

One such dispute developed when a foreman told an employee on the night shift to go home because of an offense the man committed. Before the worker left, a night superintendent entered the discussion and in effect overrode the foreman's authority. He gave the employee a written reprimand and, after exacting a promise from him to do a better job, directed him to go back to work. Subsequently, on the request of the foreman, the matter was reopened, and the penalty of discharge was assessed. [44] The facts of this case presented a strong reason for a finding of double jeopardy.

The next example is typical of cases in which unions argue for the application of this concept. A foreman discovered a man sleeping. The evidence that the employee had left his work post for this purpose was convincing. He therefore appeared to have deliberately violated a well-known plant rule that had been consistently enforced. The foreman woke him and told him to get back on the job, and then went to his office to think the matter over. He knew that only the plant manager had discharge authority. The offense was later discussed among management representatives, and the decision was made to discharge the employee. In commenting on the union's protest of double jeopardy, Arbitrator Paul M. Hebert remarked:

> If, therefore, the facts established that C_____ had been disciplined, that discipline, even though inadequate, would be final and the matter could not be reported. The facts before us make the doctrine of double jeopardy inapplicable because it is quite clear from the evidence that [the Foreman] took no disciplinary action but merely made his report upon which the subsequent action was taken. [The Foreman's] talk with C_____ was not intended as nor was it a reprimand or disciplinary action. It is true that C_____ testified that he thought he was disciplined. But his testimony was not convincing as to what the discipline consisted of. This was necessarily so for there was in fact no discipline other than the discharge itself. The plea of double jeopardy is without merit and cannot be sustained under the facts of this case. [45]

There is another and similar sequence of events about which unions frequently raise this same issue. For example, an employee was absent from his work station for an hour and a half. He refused to explain his whereabouts, and in an interview with the plant superintendent, he used extremely abusive and obscene language and threatened him repeatedly with bodily harm. He was then advised to go home and report the next morning to the personnel office for a final disposition of his case. When he appeared the next day, he exhibited the same defiant and belligerent attitude and was told he was discharged. The union asserted that management's sending the man home coupled with the discharge constituted double jeopardy. The ruling did not sustain this argument.[46]

Unions have attempted to apply the doctrine of double jeopardy to an even wider territory than these cases cover. Their arguments have often had the character of attacks against the very cornerstones of the progressive discipline concept. An employee's past record has a very material bearing on most discipline and discharge disputes. However, some unions would prohibit its introduction if possible. They argue that to consider it is to expose the grievant to double jeopardy. How arbiters have responded to such pleadings should be of interest to all practitioners in management's ranks. Arbitrator Gabriel Alexander has stated a widely held opinion in these words:

> One argument occasionally advanced in defense of employee wrongdoers is that, once a man has suffered a penalty for misconduct, he has "paid his debt to society" and thereafter is free from stigma because of previous misconduct. Corrective discipline does not accept this argument as valid. It responds with the proposition, which in my opinion has greater validity, that management is entitled to have an obedient and cooperative work-force and ought not to be subjected to the necessity for retaining in its employ persons who over a period of time demonstrate by their conduct that they cannot accommodate themselves to reasonable job rules.[47]

Generally, the concept of double jeopardy is not found applicable in discharge cases involving a series of minor offenses when management has imposed corrective discipline properly.[48] Corrective discipline is progressive. Unless the employee's offense is so grave as to merit immediate discharge, the degree of punishment will be decided by how often he has erred before and how important the rule is that he has broken. A first offender guilty of a minor infraction of a rule is given a minor punishment, perhaps an oral warning or a written reprimand. If he breaches a similar or comparable rule on a second occasion within a reasonable time, a more serious penalty will usually be assessed. Further violations will prompt harsher and harsher penalties, up to and including discharge. Each severer penalty is telling the worker that the gravity of his misconduct is increasing, and each affords him another opportunity to improve so that the terminal point of discharge may be avoided.

Each step probably constitutes a grievable situation, and every discipline imposed by the employer must stand the test of just cause. If the union challenges it unsuccessfully or lodges no grievance at all, the incident becomes a part of the employee's work record. Therefore, in an arbitration hearing on a dispute, the worker's prior disciplinary record is a highly relevant consideration. Thus its introduction into the arbitration record does not expose the offending employee to any threat of double jeopardy.

INDEFINITE SUSPENSION

A disciplinary penalty that consists in a suspension from work without pay should have a beginning and an end. Reasonable though this sounds, it isn't always so. Some employers have imposed suspensions that had rather uncertain starting dates or indefinite termination points or both. A few of these cases will be reviewed here to give an idea of how arbitrators have ruled.

An employer gave a group of workers an "employee warning record" for refusing or failing to work overtime; the warning read: "You have violated the terms of the Company-Union agreement and are subject to disciplinary action. You will be given a disciplinary layoff, effective at the discretion of the Company." [49] The date for the commencement of the suspension was not fixed, its duration was not indicated, and therefore its terminal date couldn't have been more indefinite. Arbitrator Carl R. Schedler concluded likewise, and his reactions reflect the judgment of the majority of his professional colleagues:

I find that these disciplinary layoffs becoming effective at some uncertain time in the future are void and I have ordered that they be withdrawn and cancelled. The evidence adduced from the Company's chief witness indicates that the penalties may be invoked at any time in the future and that the amount of the penalty was still uncertain but would probably be five days. In other words, the Company might next week, next month, or next year decide to activate the layoff. So far as I know, such a practice is unknown in industrial relations, and I cannot sanction it in the absence of specific agreement. Agreed-upon delays pending investigation and discussion are one thing; further uncertain delays, not agreed upon, after the occurrence of the incident are quite another. To impose the penalty at some later date might give rise to the assumption that it was being imposed for some subsequent misconduct and not for the initial incident and thus create and compound difficult problems. Furthermore, disciplinary action in an industrial establishment is taken for corrective purposes. It is to serve notice on the employee that he must correct the situation or possibly suffer further inconvenience. Corrective discipline serves as a warning and not necessarily as a penalty. Even an employee properly discharged for an offense is put on notice that he must correct his ways in his next place of employment if he is to continue on the job. A sort of "suspended sentence" hanging over an employee's head is contrary to all usual methods of corrective discipline.[50]

Similar rulings are found in other cases. For example, a worker is guilty of insubordination. As a penalty, the employer directs him to go home and not return until he is willing to comply with the order. Or an employee offends a management representative with abusive or obscene remarks. The employer feels this is disruptive to efficient operations and sends the man home, telling him not to come back until he is willing to apologize and behave. Such actions will not be supported by arbitral rulings.

The purpose of the discipline is to correct the offender's conduct. In the occurrences described, the employer's presumption should be that the action has served its purpose when the worker returns following a suspension of a stipulated period. If the insubordinate or abusive employee continues his improper behavior thereafter, he is subject to further disciplinary action for repeating the offense, up to and including discharge.

Another fault of this form of suspension should be noted. Unless its duration is clearly stated, the employer is leaving its term to the discretion of the offender. Workers should not be left to decide their own punishment. The responsibility for assessing the proper degree of penalty rests solely with the employer. He has failed to meet that responsibility unless he clearly declares the beginning and terminal dates of the discipline.

Off-the-Job Misconduct

The News Syndicate Co., Inc. was involved in a criminal case against two of its employees. Federal agents entered its premises and arrested the employees on the charge of collecting bets without having purchased a federal tax stamp. The company was not notified that the men would be arrested or that they were under surveillance until immediately before the arrests. The management then decided that they should be suspended pending determination of their guilt or innocence. The union grieved. The arbitrator agreed that suspension was an eligible action with employees accused of such a crime. This was particularly so because the information rested solely with the law enforcement officials and was not available to the company and because the evidence indicated that the crime of which the employees were accused took place on company premises.

The real question that arose, however, was how long such a suspension might go on. Arbitrator Monroe Berkowitz resolved this quandary and remarked on it as follows:

> This suspension has now continued for more than three months. This begins to be an extreme length of time for the employees to be placed in a position where they are neither receiving their normal salaries nor have they been cut off from all future chances of employment with the Company. It is likely that when the suspension was originally imposed the expectations of the Company were that this matter would be disposed of before this. Although it is certainly not the fault of the Company that the trial of these employees has been delayed, it must be recognized that we are dealing with a serious matter where the freedom of these employees is at stake, and in these situations delays are sometimes inevitable. . . .
>
> In light of the amount of time that has elapsed since the imposition of the suspensions and the nature of the evidence against them presently available to the Company, the Arbitrator finds that it is neither fair nor just to continue these employees in this state of economic limbo. They should be returned to their positions with the Company, but without back pay. This vacating of the suspensions is done without prejudice to the right of the Company to institute discharge proceedings at any time and particularly once further evidence about the nature of their offense on February 14 comes into possession.[51]

What an employee does on his own time and outside the business premises is normally his own affair. Also, violation of criminal laws is not per se just cause for disciplinary action. But arbitrators will often uphold a suspension if a criminal charge pending against an employee threatens to impair his usefulness to the employer and affect business.

The employer's customer relations were a consideration in the next case involving a food store employee who was picked up and charged with receiving stolen property. The next morning, released on bond, he was advised by the store manager that he would have to be suspended. The union grieved, and at the hearing it argued that a man should be presumed innocent until proved guilty, that the charge was dismissed in court, and that the employee had therefore been suspended without just cause. The arbitrator agreed with the union's first proposition but held that it missed the point. The question was not one of guilt or innocence; "Rather, the question is whether Management has the right to suspend an employee whose ability to provide the services for which he was hired has been substantially impaired, regardless of whether the impairment was due to any fault of the employee." [52]

The importance of public relations in a retail business is obvious. Regardless of the legal presumption of innocence, the usual customer views with suspicion any person who has been charged with a crime. It might not be too remote an analogy to compare the position of the accused to the predicament of a person who has a health problem that makes him an undesirable employee for the public to do business with. Here the grievant was charged with a crime involving moral turpitude. As has been implied, the arbiter upheld the employer's action.

The outcome of this case is consistent with established arbitral opinion. Other practitioners have repeatedly recognized that where criminal charges against an employee could reasonably be expected to affect the affairs of a company, it may properly suspend him pending court action. [53]

Similarly, Arbitrator Vernon L. Stouffer held that an employer was justified in suspending an employee convicted on a charge of indecency pending final determination of an appeal. However, he did not agree to let the suspension go on indefinitely. He sustained it in part and denied it in part, ruling as follows:

> . . . the Company had just cause to suspend the Grievant pending final court determination of his guilt. Discharge temporarily set aside pending such determination. If on such final court determination, Grievant is found innocent, discharge shall be permanently set aside and Grievant reinstated within a reasonable time not exceeding 30 days thereafter, but without back pay. If conviction is finally sustained, discharge shall again become effective. [54]

This would be the conclusion of most arbitrators. If there is legitimate reason to believe that the employee's presence in the place of work will affect efficiency or business negatively, it has customarily been held that the interim until the court disposes of the case, if not unduly long, is a reasonable suspension period. However, the equities in such situations, as in all other issues submitted to arbitration, are determined by the particular facts of each case.

PROCEDURAL REQUIREMENTS

Whatever the merits of a disciplinary penalty in itself, it may be held inappropriate for reasons of procedural defect. The fault often arises in the notification process.

Some labor agreements contain a requirement that notice be given to an employee, the union, or both before certain disciplinary actions are taken by the employer. Such was the case in the contract between Northern California Grocers Association and the Retail Clerks Union. Section IV, on discharges and layoffs, read: "Before a regular employee is discharged for incompetency or failure to perform work as required, he shall receive a written warning (with a copy to the Union), and be given an opportunity to improve his work. Notices and warnings shall become null and void after six months from date of issue." [55] A grievance was filed under this provision because the organization did not deliver the two copies of the written warning before discharging an employee who failed to follow rules for check cashing. It contended that it had warned the employee orally after his first breach of company policy that the next violation would mean his dismissal.

The arbitrator did not agree that this sufficed. The written notice requirement appeared in the contract without qualification, so that management had no right to substitute some other form of notice. This was so despite the fact that the employee was made aware of the complaint relating to his work. The end result was that the employer was found in violation of the agreement, and the arbiter ordered the reinstatement of the grievant to his job with back pay from the date of his discharge.

This is not an uncommon holding in cases of this type.

Where a contract contains a regulatory provision like the one quoted above, arbitrators have been resolute in their attitude on management's compliance with the terms. Some have considered the procedural stipulations so compelling that the employer's failure to deliver a requisite copy of the written warning to the union has been ground enough to void an otherwise valid discharge. Arbitrator Ralph C. Barnhart expressed his view on this issue as follows:

> The Union officials, if they are to function effectively, need to know what the Employer claims the facts to be as well as the employee's side of the story. It would seem to the Arbitrator that the Company would best serve its own interests in such cases in getting the story to the Union in its own words. . . .

The Arbitrator has no difficulty in ruling that where requirements of written notice involve so little burden upon the normal functioning of today's business and are actually almost second nature in the business world, and where the postal service provides return receipt service at modest cost, there would seem too slight justification for requiring less than full compliance with the Agreement. An employee's job ought not to be forfeited for failure of a procedure that costs but $.30.[56]

A similar ruling culminated a case involving McKesson & Robbins, Inc. (now Foremost-McKesson, Inc.), where the employee was reinstated with back pay. The arbiter made the award without considering the merits of the discharge on the ground that the employer had violated the contract requirement for written warnings to the union and the employee.[57]

The arbitral philosophy behind this and many other similar findings can perhaps best be expressed this way. The written notice tells the employee of his shortcomings in a formal and impressive manner. He is enabled to respond affirmatively before the problem becomes so large that the company must discharge him. It may enable the company to save the time and money it has invested in training him. It solicits the aid of the union in correcting a temporarily faltering employee, although the union's real purpose in wanting the notice is to have the opportunity of standing behind and counseling the employee when he is in conflict with management.

One cannot argue with the decisions cited above or others like them. Where the employer has negotiated a procedural requirement that is a requisite antecedent to its taking some action, it should respect that arrangement. Moreover, advising employees of its complaints regarding their work performance is a preliminary to harsher discipline that management has an ethical obligation to carry out. Such a step is an intrinsic part of the progressive correction process. An employee should never be caught unaware when he is penalized. He should know why it is happening, which means that he should be informed of all management's complaints that precede it at the times they arise.

However, there are persuasive objections to management's being constrained by contractual commitment to put the notification of impending discipline in writing and to involve the union in the correction of employees.

On the first point, the situations and circumstances that call for discipline are too numerous and varied to be anticipated. By committing itself to giving prior written notice, management may be handcuffing itself unrealistically. Too often management must step up to an incident swiftly. The requirement of written notification can prevent it from doing so. It can compromise the employer's right of managerial discretion and action and materially reduce the available alternatives. It certainly constitutes another form of restriction on the company's right to manage the business.

On the second point, communication with the union as an institution is very desirable—in fact, essential. But maintaining order in the working place is not the responsibility of the union. That responsibility resides solely with management. The experienced practitioner knows the many arguments unions put forward in negotiating to obtain such a contract clause. The major thesis is that they can thereby assist management with problem employees. They can help straighten them out; they can talk to them more effectively than company representatives can.

It is true that the union sometimes does actually help or rehabilitate an employee headed down the wrong road, but this is relatively rare. As was pointed out earlier, the union's basic purpose in inserting such a contract clause is to guarantee it the opportunity of being at hand when an employee is facing trouble with management. In most cases, the union is much more interested in representing the employee's than the employer's interests—and that is as it should be. Thus management should not delude itself into believing that agreeing to a contractual provision of this sort will supply it with a helpmate in the union. Nor should it be willing to share its responsibility for maintaining proper behavior and adherence to reasonable procedures and rules of order.

Chapter 4

Reasons for Discipline or Discharge: On-the-Job Factors

The activities for which employees are disciplined are far too numerous to be covered fully. To list them all and review some cases relevant to each would be a staggering undertaking, impossible to carry out within a single volume. What will be attempted here is a review of the kinds of situations that employers experience most commonly.

This chapter will discuss factors that directly affect the employee's work. The activities treated in Chapter 5 impinge on his usefulness in his job by impairing his relationship with his company.

ABSENTEEISM

Employers have a right to expect attendance with some degree of regularity from their employees. As Chapter 1 explained briefly, companies spell out this right in various terms. A Dayton Steel Foundry Company rule, for example, cites absences without proper reasons as minor infractions that will evoke a written warning for the first offense, one- and three-day suspensions for the second and third, and discharge for the fourth.[1] Section B of the Commercial Steel Casting Co. shop rules provides that

> Repeated unauthorized absenteeism will be cause for dismissal at the discretion of the Management on repeated occurrences after the employee

has been notified by his Foreman that the offense has been committed. A permanent record of the notification [Discipline Notice] shall be incorporated in the personnel record of the employee at the time it is given. The fourth Discipline Notice for the same offense within 12 months will result in a one-week layoff; the fifth will result in discharge.[2]

Arbitrators recognize and stand behind the general principle that management may discipline for absenteeism. Whether a given penalty is upheld depends on a number of variables. Were prior warnings or notice required, and if so, were they given? What is the employee's record of attendance and discipline? Has the employer meted out discipline for this offense consistently? What are the surrounding circumstances?[3]

Although the reasons supplied by an employee for each absence may be valid and legitimate, he may still be disciplined for excessive absenteeism. One word of caution should be issued in this connection: arbiters generally hold that a worker must be put on notice and given an opportunity to improve before finally being discharged.[4] His record, incidentally, will include failures to work on an overtime day if he had agreed to work. These constitute absences for which he may be disciplined and are generally treated the same way as absences on regular workdays.[5]

In upholding the discharge of a Metal Salts Corp. employee who was tardy approximately 25 percent of the time, Arbitrator Whitley P. McCoy expressed the preponderant arbitral viewpoint on excessive absenteeism as well: Where an employee is absent so much, even with the best reasons, that her services are of no value to the Company, she cannot be expected to remain in the Company's employ."[6] The same arbiter was called upon to hear a later case, at the Westinghouse Electric Corp., and said in his finding: "Repeated absences, over a long period of time, even if [for] valid reasons such as genuine illnesses, may make an employee of so little value, if not an actual handicap to the Company, as to justify a severance of the employment relation."[7]

Arbitrator Roy R. Ray decided a case in which he called the grievant's record of absences and tardiness one of the worst he had ever seen. The statistics speak for themselves:

During the 10-month period preceding his discharge he was absent 23.5% of the work days, tardy 40.2% of the remainder and left work early on 5.9% of the days, for a total of 69.6%. He had, in effect, become only a part-time employee and an unreliable one at that. Though repeatedly counselled concerning his attendance record, forcefully warned on March 4 and given a written warning on March 13, his record did not improve.

He was absent, late or had incomplete days on 66.7% of the work days during the period of March 5 through March 28, and was late on the last three days he worked, March 26, 27 and 28. This record clearly warranted the [Company's terminating] the grievant's service.[8]

Companies frequently use percentage as well as number of absences to support their position in arbitration cases. Discharge was upheld, for example, on the evidence of the following figures presented in cases selected at random:

1. Absent 47 times, or 17 percent of the time, in one year.[9]
2. Absent an average of 39.3 percent of the time per year.[10]
3. Absent from 6.5 to 100 percent of the time in a seven-year period.[11]
4. Absent 33 times in one year.[12]
5. Absent or tardy 26 percent of the time.[13]
6. Absent an average of once every nine shifts.[14]
7. Absent without medical excuse 22 times and tardy 35 times in a 16-month period.[15]
8. Absent 22 percent of the time over 14 years.[16]
9. Absent 50 percent of the scheduled workdays.[17]
10. Worked only 54 percent of the available hours.[18]

Arbitrator Walter G. Seinsheimer, deciding a case involving the Gartland-Haswell Foundry Co. in August 1965, quoted from absenteeism rate data for industry as a whole. The average for male workers was somewhere between 4 and 4.5 percent.[19] However, managements should not rely too heavily on national averages when defending a disciplinary action for this offense. Most arbitrators would question the meaningfulness of the figures in a dispute arising at a specific company or plant. The figure can be high in Detroit and low in Dallas, high in one industry and low in another, high in winter and low in summer, and so forth.[20]

Mitigating Circumstances

When should exculpatory reasons mitigate the penalty of discharge? The Taft Broadcasting Company fired an employee for excessive absenteeism. The union argued that special circumstances, such as the employee's race, her relationship with other employees, and her home situation, had to be considered in the evaluation of just cause. The arbitrator, James V. Altieri, rejected this contention since the excessive absenteeism had admittedly occurred, it justified her termination regardless of the cause, and the penalty was not shown to be connected with any other punitive motive. He held that only if the primary issue were related to the mitigating circumstances would they be relevant.[21]

Arbitrator Thomas T. Purdom fashioned a unique remedy in resolving an absenteeism dispute. He first ruled that the company was justified in discharging an employee guilty of excessive absences during the two years preceding the present case. The employee had a health problem and had received doctor's orders to lose weight and stop smoking. It appeared that the employer had cooperated fully with him and the union regarding his health problem, but to no avail—his absenteeism continued.

A stipulation agreed to at the beginning of the hearing gave the arbiter great discretion, empowering him to reach a disposition that would have otherwise been impossible; without this latitude, he would have sustained the discharge and dismissed the grievance. The employee's work record before the past two years showed only four or five absences in 16 years. In view of this, the arbiter ruled that the worker could elect to take a leave of absence and return to work with full seniority if within 18 months he lost 150 pounds, stopped smoking, and obtained a doctor's certificate stating that he was able to take up his job again. His failure to meet these requirements within the allotted time would result in the permanent termination of his employment.[22]

DAMAGE TO OR LOSS OF MATERIALS

Employees are often disciplined for damaging or losing tools, equipment, or materials. For the action to be sustained, the damage or loss must be deemed to have been within the worker's control. Also, he must have been fully aware of his responsibilities with regard to the property.

The employee's action need not have been deliberate; it can have been negligent or careless. In either case, the burden of proof rests with the employer. Of course, if it is established that the damage or loss was intentional, a severer penalty will probably be upheld.

Negligent Acts

An employee failed to shut off a water valve at the right time, so that water spilled over and shorted out an electric motor. The resulting power failure caused a 50 percent reduction in operations for five hours. Turning off the water valve was a regular part of the job of this worker, who also had a previous record of discipline. The company imposed a two-week suspension for negligence, and the arbitrator upheld the action.[23]

An employee of Byerlite Co. of Koppers Co., Inc. was also held to have been properly discharged for negligence. While in charge of certain tanks that were being filled, he failed to cut off the intake in time to prevent excessive flow or overflow because he did not notice warning signs or take customary precautions.[24]

In an Ideal Cement Company case, a kiln burner closing down the kiln failed to take proper steps to reduce heat after the temperature in the kiln rose above the danger point. This resulted in serious damage to the equipment. The employee was discharged for gross negligence. The arbiter ruled that the evidence supported the charge, and in view of the fact that the employee had a record of two prior reprimands for sleeping on the job, he upheld the employer's action as having been taken for proper cause.[25]

Discharges have been reduced to temporary layoffs in instances where the employees have excellent work records or are on new jobs. These conditions were inapplicable in the cases just cited. The employees had ample familiarity with their tasks and had received discipline for related reasons previously.

Deliberate Acts

Where management takes action against employees for willful damage to company property, it bears a special obligation to prove its allegation. So the Publishers Association of New York City (*The New York Times*) discovered in a dispute with the New York Stereotypers Union.

A supervisor was observing an employee from some distance behind him. The man, visible only from the waist up, was making arm and body movements that appeared to be directed toward a piece of equipment in front of him. Several months before, he had been disciplined for willfully damaging company property. After watching him for a minute, the supervisor approached him, but on reaching the equipment he found him applying oil to the machine, a normal job responsibility. However, operating switches and fuses were found to be damaged, and the man was summarily discharged.

At the arbitration hearing, the foreman testified to what he had witnessed. The claim was that the worker had caused the damage to the machine, although it was admitted that the arm and body movements were akin to those of someone who was merely oiling it. The company's case, then, was based primarily on surmise. The union declined to present any evidence, arguing only that the company had failed to provide a prima facie case for its allegation. The arbiter agreed, and the man was reinstated with full back pay.[26]

In contrast to this decision is one that came out of a dispute at the General Electric Company. Arbitrator Donald A. Crawford rejected a union contention that the testimony of the company's eyewitness was not sufficiently convincing to support the decision handed down. Arbiter Crawford commented:

> The Arbitrator cannot agree with the conclusion. H_____ was a very impressive witness. His location gave him an excellent view of what was going on below him including the Grievant's performance of his work. Nothing in the normal performance of the Grievant's duties would require him to strike the front right-hand side of the porcelain liner with a sharp blow of a hammer. Completely to the contrary, the fragile nature of the inner lining (glass) required that any work with a hammer, such as moving excess foam adhering to the liner or testing a "pimple," would be done carefully and gently—not by a sharp hammer blow. And H_____'s description of the blow was that of a sharp blow, not one that could be mistaken for tapping excess foam away with his putty knife, or for an accidental dropping of his hammer, or for letting his arm fall to hit an already dented area.[27]

The difference between the General Electric case and *The New York Times* matter is obvious. The *Times* foreman reported what he presumed he saw; the GE foreman reported what he witnessed firsthand from a clear vantage point.

At Quick Industries, Inc., sabotage and pranks had beset an assembly line for several weeks. The foreman had warned the assembly-line workers on various occasions that the trouble must stop, and the job superintendent had told them that the line would be shut down and they would be sent home if these acts continued. The incidents were causing a substantial disruption of production, loss of time, and consequently expense to the company. The discussions with the employees were of no avail. Finally, 12 of them were sent home an hour and a half before the end of their shift one day.

None of the facts just outlined was in dispute, and there was no question that the acts constituted just cause for discipline of the guilty. But before the test of just cause can be applied, adequate proof of the guilt of the person or persons involved must be established. This was not the case here. The arbiter was not unsympathetic to the gravity of the company's problem. But in his well-reasoned opinion, he stated that he believed he would be doing a disservice to the parties and would be violating a basic concept of American justice if he permitted a dismissal of this grievance.[28]

Justice William O. Douglas, referring to a Supreme Court decision, has written: "Guilt by association is a dangerous doctrine. It condemns one man for the unlawful conduct of another"; and again: "The almanac of liberty for the free world is filled with episodes where the means are plowed though the ends sought are worthy." [29]   The American system of law comes from English common law as well as from statutes, and is based on a centuries-old concept that "it is better that ten guilty persons escape than that one innocent suffer."

These were the sentiments expressed by Arbitrator Jerome Gross in the above dispute. Their tenor was characteristic of him, and it can be found in the remarks of other jurists and teachers and in other citations of published labor arbitration reports.

DISHONESTY

The term "dishonesty" is used here to mean misconduct that involves either money or property. It goes beyond misappropriation or theft— to be reviewed further on in this chapter as a separate issue—in that it includes any conduct that tends to perpetrate a fraud on an employer resulting in financial loss. Some contracts actually define dishonesty and may even specify what would be considered dishonest acts. A list of abuses in this category would include taking or giving bribes, misusing company records, tampering with vending machines, padding expense reports, and using company funds for personal purposes. Falsifying work records or information on job applications, like theft, is troublesome and common enough to warrant separate treatment also; it will be taken up later.

Such dishonest acts as these, among others, have been established as providing just cause for discipline or discharge. The burden of proof rests with the employer, as always, and the punishment must be timely and befit the employee's work record. Because a charge of dishonesty reflects upon a person's character and standing in society at large, the evidence presented by the charging party, the employer, must be fully persuasive.

A company's failure to follow a long-established practice of notifying the union before firing an employee for dishonesty may be considered such a breach of procedure as to provoke an arbitrator to reinstate the worker. With some arbiters, the fact that the employee was caught red-handed may modify such an order. It has also been held that where the contract required the company to inform both the employee and the union within 72 hours of receiving evidence of the employee's dishonesty, the company could not postpone the notification while it gathered additional evidence.

DRINKING

Almost all employers have a rule prohibiting employees from drinking on the job or reporting for work in an intoxicated condition, and probably no arbitrator would question management's right to enforce these prohibitions. But arbiters often rule that discharge is too severe a penalty, particularly for a first offense by an employee with a good work record and in the absence of convincing evidence that his condition prevented him from performing his job.[30]

Where the employee is in personal contact with the public at the time of the offense, a discharge for drinking is more likely to be upheld. This is also true when the job is such that drinking will endanger the safety of others, as in the case of truck driving.[31] In these instances arbitrators seem to apply a stricter standard.

Without doubt, it is critical that persons under the influence of alcohol be kept from behind a steering wheel. Therefore, a relatively low percentage of alcohol in the blood may be considered more dangerous in a driver than in a nondriver. For example, Sweden normally fines anyone found driving with an alcohol concentration exceeding 0.08 percent in the blood and sends those whose count surpasses 0.15 percent to jail. Norway punishes all who have a concentration exceeding 0.05 percent; the figure in Denmark is 0.10 percent. Many American states accept an alcohol concentration above 0.15 percent as prima facie proof of driving while under the influence of alcohol. Many authorities who assert that 0.15 percent is too high for normal purposes nonetheless urge an even lower figure in traffic cases, since they find that not only judgment but visual acuity and resistance to glare are affected long before visible signs of intoxication appear.

Claiming that an employee is intoxicated and proving it are two different things. As usual, and as it should be, the burden of proof rests with the company when it makes such an accusation. The tests that establish the degree of intoxication, however, are not always available to or utilized by the employer. Therefore, some companies have taken to approaching the problem from a safer side.

Recognizing the complications of according with the burden of proof doctrine, an employer who firmly believes a worker intoxicated may instead discipline or discharge him on the ground that he reported or is working "under the influence of intoxicants." To be "intoxicated" denotes loss of control of one's physical and mental faculties. To be "under the influence" denotes a lesser but appreciable effect on one's physical and mental powers because of alcoholic intake. In disputes over discipline based on this charge, the union often argues that what the employee does on his own time and while away from the plant is his business. This general statement is correct, but it has certain recognized limitations. When the employee's off-duty activities affect his performance of his job, then the conduct becomes a matter with which the employer may be properly concerned, as we will see in some detail in the next chapter. Thus an employee who reports for work in a condition that does not allow him to do it properly is falling short of the obligations on him inherent in the employer-employee relationship.[32]

An especially cautious management that felt it had to discipline a worker for drinking might avoid even the phrase "under the influence" and rather base its action on a claim that he was in an "unfit" or "unsuitable condition" to perform his job. Indicia would be slurred speech, uncoordinated movements, staggering and a poor sense of balance, glazed eyes, rumpled clothes, an antagonistic manner, and so forth. A company using this approach trusts the arbitrator will deem signs like these to be evidence that the worker was temporarily incapacitated, without its needing to prove that they were the product of an inebriated state.

Efforts to Prove Intoxication

In the following case, the employer might have been well advised to use one of these alternate strategies. The Federal Services, Inc. discharged a plant guard for intoxication while on duty on the basis of witnesses' statements that the guard's lips were dry and that he burped. Although one observer "smelled no alcohol" and "didn't see him stagger," the guard was "a little unsteady on his feet and in his talk," and "something was obviously wrong" with him. All the company's witnesses testified that, in their best judgment, the grievant was intoxicated. However, it was the opinion of the arbiter that the facts they related were insufficient to justify their conclusion. He commented:

> Intoxication at work, particularly in a position as important and critical as that of a guard at an important defense installation, cannot be tolerated. But this does not lessen the requirement that the burden of proving a charge of this nature (intoxication) is on the Company, nor does it mean that in every case of suspected intoxication the Company need impose the supreme penalty of discharge. . . .
>
> The question of the Grievant's sobriety could readily have been documented had the Company sent the Grievant to a local hospital or other proper place for a sobriety test. By not doing this, in the face of the Grievant's and the Union's readiness to voluntarily submit the Grievant to such a test, the Company elected to base its case against the Grievant on the sound judgment of its own officials. And while they no doubt were entirely honest in their belief that the Grievant was intoxicated, other equally honest and competent observers held an opposite view.[33]

The grievant was reinstated in his job with back pay for all time lost. There is probably no recorded case that could provide a better example of why some employers have chosen to avoid the specific allegation that an employee is intoxicated.

Even when a company attempts to establish a charge of intoxication through a sobriety test, it may experience complications. In the following case, the company learned that it had not proved its allegation even though it had established that the worker's alcohol consumption exceeded generally accepted norms.

Kaiser Steel Corporation discharged an employee for intoxication whose blood test showed a 0.19 percent alcohol content. The sobriety scale used by the employer and many states sets the rating of 0.15 percent or more as conclusive evidence of intoxication. Arbitrator J. A. C. Grant overturned the discharge and ordered the grievant's reinstatement on these grounds: (1) the employee demonstrated no other clinical symptoms of intoxication, (2) medical authorities warn against accepting a specific rating as an index of intoxication without reference to other clinical symptoms, and (3) the employee was a heavy drinker and, according to medical opinion, could tolerate a higher concentration of alcohol in the blood than the average person without becoming intoxicated.

The medical literature referred to by this arbitrator includes the reprint files of the Alcohol Clinic of the Department of Psychiatry, the Medical School of the University of California at Los Angeles; 19 volumes of the *Quarterly Journal of Studies on Alcohol* (QJSA), published regularly since 1940; and a number of authoritative treatises such as Louis S. Goodman and Alfred Gilman's *The Pharmacological Basis of Therapeutics* (second edition, 1955). Arbitrator Grant's discussion is instructive for the extensive research it exhibits and thus warrants quoting at some length:

> Many studies have confirmed that the effects of alcohol on the central nervous system are more marked when the concentration in the blood is rising rather than falling. Similarly, when the alcohol concentration is increased and maintained following intoxication, the symptoms of intoxication disappear in from 4 to 10 hours at blood [alcohol] levels even higher than those at which they developed. In short, apparently the central nervous system acquires in time an ability to function more effectively at a given concentration of alcohol. Further evidence that a real tissue tolerance for alcohol develops is furnished by studies that have compared habitual heavy drinkers with moderate drinkers. Goodman and Gilman state, p. 106, that "The repeated use of alcohol results in the development of tolerance, and larger doses must then be taken in order to procure characteristic effects. . . . The alcohol addict still has an upper limit of tolerance, which is usually only 3 or 4 times the amount of alcohol that can be taken by the occasional drinker." Goldberg's studies on tolerance, summarized in J. H. Gaddam, *Lectures on the Scientific Basis of Medicine* (1954–55), vol. 4, p. 241, indicate that "A given degree of intoxication would cost the average heavy drinker about 2.5 times as much as it would cost the average abstainer." Jetter's studies, summarized *id.* at p. 247 (and see QJSA, vol. 3, pp. 475 ff.), showed that the toughest 10% of his subjects could stand 5 times as much alcohol as the 10% with the weakest heads. Dr. Rabinowitch, writing in the *Canadian Bar Review* for 1951, vol. 31, p. 1072, states: "I have seen intoxication . . . with values as low as 0.05%. . . . On the other hand, I have also seen persons with alcohol levels of 0.168%. 0.21%, 0.273% and higher who showed no evidence of intoxication." (See also QJSA, vol. 2, p. 35 [1941].)
>
> Mirsky, Piker, Rosenbaum, and Lederer, in their study of "Adaptation of the Central Nervous System to Varying Concentrations of Alcohol in the Blood," QJSA, vol. 2, p. 35 and pp. 43–44 (1941), concluded that the evidence "casts considerable doubt on the validity of the use of the alcohol concentration in the blood as an index of intoxication. It is apparent that, given a blood alcohol [concentration] of 200 mg. percent (0.20% on the Company's scale) or higher, the only deduction that is permissible is that the subject may have been drunk at some time up to the moment the blood sample was drawn, and not necessarily that the subject was drunk at that moment." . . . Goodman and Gilman, p. 106,

conclude that generally an alcohol concentration of 0.20% "is associated with mild to moderate intoxication. In some individuals, of course, this level does not indicate drunkenness, and it must be viewed merely as an average. Obviously, the laboratory data must be interpreted in the light of results of clinical examination." Loftus reached the same conclusion after a study of all automobile drivers in Oslo, Norway, examined over a period of 15 years because of police suspicions. See the translation of his report in QJSA, vol. 18, pp. 217 ff. (1957). He also recognized that he was dealing with a "loaded sample," i.e., "those who have behaved in such a way as to attract the attention of the police. The percentage of persons diagnosable [as] not sober is likely to be higher in such a sample than in an average group with corresponding blood alcohol levels." (*Id.* at p. 228.) ` . . .

It should be stressed that the reports upon which the Company relies for its 0.15% test were intended to apply only in the case of automobile drivers. Even those reports, to quote from the National Safety Council, warned us, "The results of a chemical analysis should not be the sole criterion upon which an official judgment is based. The results of a chemical test should be employed to confirm conclusions drawn from clinical and physical diagnoses. It is also emphasized that arbitrary deductions based upon the so-called '0.15% percent line demarcation' be avoided." As the British Medical Association stated in its 1954 report . . . at p. 22: "The responses of different individuals to the same concentration of alcohol in the tissues vary widely. General statements cannot be safely applied in individual cases; neither should a diagnosis rely solely on the results of laboratory tests. An examining practitioner should base his opinion in the first instance solely on his clinical findings, modified subsequently, if necessary, in the light of the results of any laboratory tests." [34]

FALSIFICATION

Arbitrators appear to agree generally that some discipline is warranted when an employee is proved to have falsified time or production records or employment applications. However, it must be shown that the act was a deliberate one with intent to defraud rather than a mere oversight or lapse of memory.

False Work and Production Records

The distortion of a work record may manifest itself in a variety of ways, ranging from manipulation of time cards to misrepresentation of production counts.

A union steward's time card was punched earlier than the time he actually came in, but the steward contended he himself had punched the card at the earlier hour. Despite the fact that he may not have been to blame initially, it was held that the company could fire him because he knowingly became a party to the violation by permitting it. In another case, an employer was held to have properly fired an employee for punching the card of a fellow worker along with his own when no explanation was provided for the fact that both cards had been punched at the same time and the other man had not punched his own.[35]

The misrepresentation may involve work time during the day. At the General Electric Company, a union shop committee chairman persisted in marking on his production work slip time that he had actually spent on union business and should have indicated on a separate slip. The contract contained specific provisions relating to time that union officials spent during working hours on union business and limiting the amount that would be paid for. The union officer had been warned about this practice on several occasions by a number of supervisors and officials of the company before he was disciplined with a one-week layoff. Arbitrator Daniel Kornblum upheld the suspension.[36]

Falsifying a production record does more than increase a company's direct overhead dishonestly. Among other things, it distorts inventory records and production costs, interferes with scheduling and the equitable allocation of work assignments, impedes the development of fair performance credits and earning opportunities, and plays havoc with the sound administration of a wage incentive plan if one exists.

One form of production falsification is "banking," or undercounting the work actually performed during a given time. This was the accusation of the Harnischfeger Corporation against an employee it discharged for failing to report production amounting to more than 24 standard hours' credit. The worker had been warned against the practice just one week earlier under a plant rule against "falsification of records, reports or applications for employment."[37] Taking the man's prior disciplinary records of suspensions and warnings for other offenses into account, Arbitrator Harold M. Gilden upheld the company's action.

At Singer Company, an employee was discharged for the opposite offense of overreporting his production count. He admitted claiming 1,600 pieces when in fact an audit found the count to be 1,382. Although the grievant was aware of his overage throughout the entire workday, he never attempted to correct his error until he saw the checker moving parts to the scale to make an audit. The arbitrator,

Sidney L. Cahn, found this timing significant, coupled with the employee's knowledge of the overage, which on too many occasions during the day he "conveniently forgot to change." The company's action was sustained.[38]

Falsified Employment Application

Falsifying a job application may be considered a somewhat different matter from distorting production or work records. The present consensus among arbitrators is that it should not be considered justification for peremptory discharge after some reasonable time; a lengthy period of satisfactory employment following the falsification is usually viewed as a bar to a subsequent discharge for that single error.[39] This is particularly true where the facts that are falsified are not of a nature to endanger present or future work relationships.

Misrepresentation on job applications seems to be a rather common practice; in fact, most employers expect applicants to highlight their strengths and good points and soft-pedal their shortcomings. However, if it involves material facts that would have led the company to find the worker unsuitable for employment, it may constitute a serious enough consideration for discharge to be justified. For example, a company could fire an employee who had omitted half his former jobs from his application and had not stated he had been sued three times if the form specifically asked for this information and warned that any falsification or omission would be cause for dismissal. One expert has stated the issue in these words:

> Arbitrators have sought past reported cases to distinguish what matters and what does not matter in falsified or omitted statements on employment applications. Minor details and slips of memory do not matter; a few days worked here or there not mentioned, the name of an elementary school wrongly given, a date far back in the past not rightly remembered [all] come under this heading. The things that matter are those that might well have led to a different decision about the hiring of an employee had the Employer known the full facts at the time. . . .[40]

A dispute involving Braniff Airways, Incorporated illustrates this principle. An employee failed to include a former employer on his employment application. This omission came to the company's attention two years later, and he was immediately discharged. Several factors influenced the arbiter's award. First, the grievant was a competent worker with a good reputation among his fellow employees. Second, he had resigned from the job he had omitted from his application, and his record there contained no serious offenses. Third, he had omitted the former employment because of a personal difficulty with his brother, who worked at the plant, and not because of any intent to deceive Braniff. The arbiter's comments in this connection are well worth review:

> It is our belief that an omission of a fact in an application which causes the Company to give a job to an unqualified applicant is a serious omission and the applicant has fraudulently secured the position. We think where an omission results in such fraud the Company is well within its rights to terminate unless it has, by its own negligence, retained the employee for such a long period of time as to raise a presumption of waiver. We think, in this case, the Company has completely failed to show that the Grievant secured his position through fraud; and, whether or not the Company would have hired him on the basis of information it might have secured from Slick Airways is, in retrospect, purely speculative. We also find from other cases that arbitrators have usually upheld termination where the applicant omitted convictions of crimes or where he failed to disclose some latent physical condition, or where he omitted to state that he had been found to be a security risk. We think that such omissions are of real consequence and, if disclosed, in most instances, would result in the applicant's failure to obtain employment. In the instant case, the Grievant did not omit any such important items. On the whole record we think the facts simply do not justify the Company's action of discharging the Grievant and we will order his reinstatement.[41]

As this decision indicated by way of example, withholding information about previous injuries and illnesses from the employment application does constitute a material omission that could justify the employer in discharging the employee.[42]

At the Diamond Power Specialty Corporation, as a case in point, an employee was discharged for having failed to give truthful answers to questions on the job application regarding former work injuries and compensation claims. It was quite clear that the grievant had not answered the questions properly or correctly. He had said that he had never applied for workmen's compensation whereas he had in fact filed eight claims with the Industrial Commission of Ohio over a three-year period. He had answered that he had no type of back injury whereas one of the claims submitted to the commission was for a strained back. In the arbiter's opinion, it was not pertinent whether the falsification was willful; since the information withheld was relevant and material, willfulness was not an element. The arbiter supported the company's action.[43]

A case involving Associated Transport, Inc. was decided the opposite way. The International Association of Machinists protested when management discharged two employees for failing to indicate any permanent physical disabilities. Arbitrator Ralph N. Campbell overturned the action on the grounds that the employees hid nothing from the company doctor, who pronounced both physically qualified, and they acted in the belief that they in fact had no permanent physical disability.[44]

FIGHTS AND ALTERCATIONS

Almost all company rules include a ban on fighting. Fights, heated arguments, and other such disturbances clearly are not conducive to plant harmony and efficiency. But unfortunately, employees do get into fights with each other and their supervisors. Some personal friction appears to be inevitable, rising out of the normal tensions of the industrial work environment. The principles espoused by labor arbitrators on this issue have established a general code of behavior that takes these considerations into account.

It is inherent in the work relationship that personnel must conform to certain well-known, commonly accepted standards of reasonable conduct while on the job.[45] Published rules and regulations are not necessary to inform an employee that misconduct such as fighting and foul language may subject him to discipline or discharge. An industrial plant is a place for the production of goods and the performance of work. While it is not a tearoom, neither is it a place for barroom conduct. Childish, uncontrolled, or irresponsible outbursts accompanied by physical or verbal assault cannot be tolerated. Such behavior is not excusable because the offender is in an agitated emotional state. When an employee lacks the emotional stability and rational judgment to restrain himself from outbursts, he also lacks the minimum qualifications to be retained as a member of the work force.[46]

One or more of the following questions will be found in most arbitral opinions on disputes over discipline for altercations: Was there one aggressor or two in the altercation? What is the employee's past work record? Was the offender's behavior provoked? If a supervisor is involved, did he provoke the employee's behavior, and did he also engage in aggressive conduct himself? If insulting and offensive words were exchanged, did they exceed the norm of shop vernacular for that institution?

The answers to such questions obviously depend on a thorough investigation of the incident by the employer. The question of whether the company has fully investigated the facts before taking disciplinary actions against fighters frequently influences an arbitrator's ruling on a particular penalty.[47]

Fighting

Where fighting has occurred, arbitrators have reduced discharges to lesser penalties when it was proved that the violence was provoked.[48] In one case, the arbiter said that it was not discriminatory for the employer to discharge the worker who initiated the assault without discharging the one who finally resorted to violence also.[49] Verbal abuse, however, is rarely considered justifiable provocation for a physical response. The laws of Ohio on assault and battery are very clear about this type of incident: "Ohio courts following the generally recognized rule have repeatedly held that mere words, however gross, abusive, and insulting or however vulgar, vile, or profane, do not justify a physical attack, and are not a defense either to a civil action for damages or to a criminal prosecution growing out of an assault and battery thus provoked." [50]

It was in this state that an arbitration hearing was held between the National Castings Corp. and the UAW concerning an altercation to which there were no witnesses. However, there was no dispute over the essential facts as related by both parties. The grievant admitted that he struck his foreman on the side of the head with his fist and then threw a 7½-pound casting after him as he retreated. The grievant claimed that the foreman had first used a racial epithet and then had dared the grievant to hit him. The foreman denied these allegations. The arbiter commented:

> Assuming the allegations of the Grievant to be true, the mere use of verbal epithets is not sufficient justification for the Grievant to use violence against his Foreman. If the epithets were used by the Foreman as the Grievant contends, the Grievant had [access] to the grievance procedure and should have used this method of bringing his allegations and accusations against the Foreman to the attention of his Union Steward and Management. In view of the circumstances, the grievance should be denied and the Grievant should not be reinstated.[51]

Most arbitrators will accord with the company position that nothing justifies a physical assault on any employee by anyone, even on the worst and most arbitrary type of supervisor. As put in one opinion, "A plant in the mainstream of production is not unlike a ship afloat. The common necessity for discipline among members of any crew upon which depends so heavily the safety and well-being of all cannot condone mutiny even against a Captain Bligh of *Bounty* notoriety." [52]

The comparison is odious, of course. In no sense are the vast majority of supervisors eligible for categorization in the Captain Bligh mold. The extreme comparison, however, does bring home the point that there are few circumstances that arbiters will consider to justify attacks on supervisors. More often than not, some penalty is upheld, though it may consist in a disciplinary measure short of discharge.

On the other hand, it is also a cardinal rule that supervisors who are attacked should do no more than is sufficient to defend themselves. They should not retaliate or fight back to the point of becoming the aggressor. They should use only the amount of force necessary to fend off the attacker, and at no time should they assume the offensive.

The ruling in the next case was predictable. The grievant was a hot-tempered employee of 14 months' service who was hypersensitive to supervisory direction. He defiantly refused to comply with a normal and reasonable work order to release cases of the company product that were stuck in the conveyor, though this was his responsibility. On being rebuked by his foreman, the grievant flew into a violent rage, knocked the supervisor to the ground, and continued to beat him until forcibly pulled away from him by others. Still unsubdued, the attacker shouted, "I'll kill him, I'll kill him." He then seized a heavy wooden case with reinforced metal corners intending to bash the dazed supervisor with it, but he was again restrained by his coworkers. The supervisor, a man of 60, was moved to a hospital for treatment of face and chest injuries. He was confined to bed for five days and to his home for another five days. At the arbitration hearing, the grievant relied exclusively on a decision rendered by the New York State Unemployment Insurance Referee Section that a worker was properly entitled to unemployment benefits because he was not guilty of misconduct in connection with his work. Needless to say, the discharge was upheld by Arbitrator Burton B. Turkus.[53]

Objectionable Language

What is abusive and offensive language? Under what circumstances will it be cause for discipline, and when will it be overlooked?

In certain types of establishments, bad language is not objectionable in itself. As a matter of fact, it may be objectionable in one portion of the business and not in another. For example, profanity may be rife among waiters in the kitchen, but they speak in a much more restrained manner in the presence of restaurant guests. Along the waterfront, in coal mines, and in garages, the choice of vocabulary is usually less than Chesterfieldian. In other words, the surroundings have a material bearing on the latitude allowed to employees in oral expression.[54]

The tone of voice and the way the language is used can also make a great deal of difference. At the American Ship Building Company, an employee told his foreman, "You're a goddamn liar and always was and will be one." The man's general attitude was belligerent, and he made the statement in the presence of a number of other employees. It even appeared that he had gone out of his way to face the foreman at a place where he had no occasion to be for any purpose. Evidence that the use of profanity between employees and supervisors was not uncommon did not preclude an arbitral finding that the employee's conduct amounted to insubordination.[55]

Another example of the effect of the manner of speaking is found in a dispute that arose at the Paragon Bridge and Steel Co. The firm employed about 600 men, and there was considerable use of profanity in the plant. Some of the phrases were obscene in the extreme. For the most part, the terms were used in normal, everyday conversational tones and were spoken in connection with conveying and acknowledging instructions.

A foreman at this plant notified an employee that he was being discharged for insubordination. Another worker then criticized the foreman for firing the man and used profanity toward him, choosing a very obscene term that suggested the foreman perform an act of indignity upon himself. The foreman told the grievant that he would be given a warning for his language and turned away to go to the office. After he had gone about six feet, the grievant called after him and repeated emphatically what he should do to himself. Several insights into arbitral philosophy are provided by the remarks this umpire made on obscene or profane language:

> Next it was contended that, as the use of obscene and profane language was customary on the part of employees and supervision, it was discriminatory to single out one employee for discharge for the use of such language. The evidence clearly established that the employees and foremen did use such terms but in an ordinary and conversational manner. They were spoken to convey directions and acknowledge instructions. But there is a vast difference between the use of such terms in an ordinary manner and in the manner which is intended to be insulting. There was abundant testimony of the use of these terms by many employees but little of instances where these words were spoken in anger. When the speaker is mad and uses such terms he intends them to be degrading and

it is an insult to the recipient. While it was customary in the plant to use such terms in ordinary conversation, it was not customary to use them in anger and with the intent [to insult] as was done in the instant case. The Grievant was not the first employee to be discharged for insubordination arising out of the use of profanity. Previously another employee had been discharged for this reason. A grievance was filed but was withdrawn by the employee before being submitted to arbitration. Presumably the employees knew that the use of obscene and profane language in a hostile manner could result in discharge.[56]

On the basis of all the facts, the arbiter held that the employer did have proper cause for discharging the grievant.

At Philco-Ford Corporation, an employee was discharged for allegedly using an obscene epithet and gesture in response to a supervisor's order. At the arbitration hearing, there was disagreement between the parties as to what had actually occurred:

The Supervisor accuses the Grievant of yelling the four-letter word, signifying coitus, [in the phrase] "_____ you, Cliff." The Grievant, while admitting that he used the four-letter word as indicated, denied that he said either "you" or "Cliff," but [claimed] that the four-letter word was merely followed by one word, i.e., "_____ it." Adding to the confusion, the Office Manager, whose office was separated from the electrical shop not only by the Foreman's office but by a hallway, testified that although he was sitting at his desk on the far side of his office, [he] distinctly heard the two words "_____ you," but said that he did not hear either the word "it" or "Cliff" amidst the din of the voices of several persons in the adjoining office and shop, where people were congregating, preparatory to leaving for the day.

Adding further to the confusion, though not brought into the discussions during any of the grievance meetings, was the insistence by the Supervisor that the Grievant had given him "the finger" as a further gesture of contempt at the time of hurling the epithet. The Grievant, on the other hand, insists that he did punctuate his remark, but only with a wave of his entire hand, which is another matter entirely.[57]

In any case, the testimony left no doubt in the mind of the arbitrator that there was an emotional outburst, along with use of an obscene word, on the grievant's part, even though it did follow a somewhat blunt and harsh order from a supervisor other than his own. The arbiter concluded that the discharge action should be reduced to a 30-day disciplinary suspension. The company had failed to conduct a full investigation of the alleged offense. Its decision was not reasonably consistent with the seriousness of the proven offense. Finally, there was no substantial evidence that this incident was anything more than a first offense and a single episode of misconduct. Therefore, even though it was of itself sufficiently serious to merit stern disciplinary action, it did not merit discharge.

Arbitrators have often taken note of the degree of influence radiating upon other employees from a man's misconduct in assessing the proper penalty. At Chrysler Corporation, for example, an employee was discharged for using abusive language in threatening a foreman. The discharge was reduced to a disciplinary layoff. The fact that no other employees were present to hear the threat made it unlikely that proper respect for foremen would be endangered by the worker's behavior.[58] A one-week suspension was held not justifiable at the Arkansas Louisiana Chemical Corporation when an employee called a plant superintendent an obscene name, since no other employee heard the exchange and the employee did not boast of it to his coworkers.[59]

GAMBLING

Most industrial establishments have rules prohibiting gambling on company premises. The reasons are obvious. Time spent in this activity is time lost from production. An employee who suffers gambling losses may take out his frustration and anger on the person he holds responsible. Morale and efficiency are always threatened. The family of the worker who experiences a substantial loss often turns to the employer for comfort and remedy. The employer is always the man in the middle under these circumstances.

Despite the existence of rules or regulations prohibiting it, gambling is prevalent in many places of work. It takes numerous forms. It may be the relatively innocuous baseball pool, check pool, or lunch-hour poker game, or it may be as serious as an organized numbers racket.

There are three basic principles arbitrators tend to observe in evaluating cases of discipline for gambling. First, the evidence connecting the employee with the gambling must be substantial and convincing.[60] Second, discharge is normally viewed as too severe a penalty for the first offense,[61] though not if the employee has been warned previously about gambling.[62] Third, and as an exception to the second principle, discharge is often considered appropriate where the employee has been connected with an organized gambling racket[63] or has engaged in gambling during working hours.[64]

At the Bethlehem Steel Company, management discharged an employee who was apprehended by plant protection officers with $400 in small bills and change and a sheet of lottery numbers. There was no question that the grievant was engaged in unlawful gambling. The fact that his activities were conducted on his own time was immaterial since they were carried out on the employer's premises. The arbiter sustained the company's action.[65]

Another employer was held to be justified in having discharged its newspaper circulation manager for organizing and participating in games run by professional gamblers. The employee knew that his gambling activities were illegal, and the company had warned him to discontinue them. His job was to supervise the work of some 30 carrier boys aged 11 to 15. The company argued that it considered a man in such a position to have a duty to the boys and their parents to maintain a moral atmosphere in the working area. Although there was no evidence that he ever corrupted the boys, it was perfectly obvious to the arbitrator that his conduct drew suspicion on him. After warning him without avail to cease his activities, the company was perfectly justified in concluding that he was not a fit and proper person to supervise boys in their formative years and that he should be discharged for the good of the operation as a whole.[66]

At the Wm. H. Haskell Mfg. Co., management had permitted a turkey raffle at Thanksgiving time for the benefit of the union's social fund and had also agreed that employees could have a World Series pool each year. On the other hand, it had a plant rule providing for immediate discharge of "any employee drinking or gambling on the Company property." Therefore, when the company discovered that a union officer was operating baseball and numbers pools at work, it discharged him. The arbiter supported this action, finding the following factors persuasive: (1) there was no evidence that the discharge was discriminatory; (2) the union officer knew he was taking a calculated risk despite his assertion that his activity was aimed at promoting sociability in the plant; and (3) the one-shot Thanksgiving turkey raffle and annual World Series pools were not comparable to the union officer's gambling schemes, which involved considerable time, daily wagers of substantial sums of money, and outside meetings with promoters of pools and thus had a generally adverse effect on plant production.[67]

HORSEPLAY AND JOKES

"Horseplay," as the term is used here, does not mean malicious conduct but rather playful activities during working hours that, like practical jokes, interfere with plant efficiency, morale, safety, or productivity. Either kind of boisterousness may be the result of chronic euphoria, or it may merely be a momentary (if rough) expression of high spirits. The problem is that too often it causes serious industrial accidents.

In judging disputes over discipline for high jinks, arbitrators are inclined to take into account whether the employee's offense was his first of its kind and what the consequences of the horseplay were. They are as concerned as management with imposing a penalty that has a salutary effect on employees who tend to be frolicsome.

For example, a company disciplined an employee who moved her supervisor's chair as the woman was about to sit down, causing her an injured back that needed a series of medical treatments. The company charged that the act was deliberate, whereas the union asserted that it was not deliberate or intended to cause harm. The arbiter agreed that discipline was warranted but did not accord with the penalty of discharge, which he felt was excessive. The employee's moving of the chair did show lack of judgment, but it was not proved to have been a malicious act. Therefore, he held that a 10-week suspension without pay would impress on the grievant that employees have obligation to "conduct themselves as mature individuals rather than as lighthearted juveniles." [68]

In a case involving Decar Plastics Corporation, the arbitrator ruled that the company was justified in discharging an employee who became aggrieved at being hit by a piece of hard rubber thrown by other employees and retaliated by placing lit cigarettes in their back pockets, though they operated machines with moving blades and entered spray booths where combustible materials were present. The grievant's conduct involved a high risk of serious injury to others and could not be considered mere horseplay. There were no mitigating circumstances. Despite union arguments, the discharge was not considered discriminatory on the basis of the company's failure to discipline other workers who engaged in horseplay without its specific knowledge. [69]

The next case concerned an employee's behavior so erotic that 14 female coworkers petitioned management to take some corrective action, and the man was discharged for indecent and untoward conduct the next day. In the ensuing grievance hearing, women employees testified to a number of incidents. One said that the grievant had followed her "to the back of the warehouse," where he had "attempted to sexually assault" her and hurt her back in the process, and that he had released her only when two other male employees were attracted to the scene after she cried out that her back was being hurt. Two other women referred also to amorous advances. The grievant denied the first allegation and dismissed the other two incidents as mere horse-play. However, the testimony of another woman at the hearing hardly supported this cavalier attitude: "About three months ago the Grievant came into the ladies' room. He tried to kiss me and tried to lay me on the couch. I told him to leave me alone but he didn't let me go, and then I yelled for the Warehouse Manager and then he let me go and then he just sat there and didn't say anything and then he left. B_____ was there; so was D_____ and E_____." [70] Another charge was that the grievant had recently called a female employee a "blond whore," a remark overheard by three male workers. Other women registered complaints that the grievant had tried to be "unduly friendly" or had made a suggestive and indecent gesture. The man insisted that all the occurrences were just bits of ordinary camaraderie.

It is interesting that despite the evil motivations attributed to the offender, none of the complainants wanted him to be discharged outright. One woman testified that if he remained in his job at the plant, her husband would not allow her to continue to work there. Another said that she was certain her husband was so outraged he would come to the plant and do serious violence to the grievant.

The arbiter nonetheless sustained the grievant's discharge as for good and sufficient cause, stating:

> The Arbitrator has recounted the salient items of testimony and proof in this record at some length because of the seriousness of the charges against the Grievant. Manifestly, an indictment of this nature should not be lightly treated; rather the Employer should be held to something like the measure of proof as obtains in a criminal trial. In this view the Arbitrator is convinced beyond a reasonable doubt that the Grievant was guilty as charged. He is persuaded that the female employees who had direct encounters with the Grievant were genuinely concerned about his misconduct, erotic and otherwise. While he is thoroughly mindful of the fact that a plant such as this is certainly not a finishing school, at the same time it is most unusual for such a sizable group of coworkers in the unit to entreat Management to do something to stop the disturbing conduct of a fellow worker and comember of the Union.[71]

INSUBORDINATION

It is presumably a well-established principle that employees are to "obey first and grieve later." Like all general principles, however, this rule has its exceptions. The presence of a labor contract compromises the implicit assumption of the authoritarian tradition that management can do nothing wrong. But, judging from management's experience in labor arbitration cases dealing with insubordination, there seems to be a carryover from the military concept of unquestioning obedience to orders. Too many employers apparently consider summary discharge the reasonable, appropriate, and necessary solution to employee acts of insubordination. To their regret these employers frequently learn that arbitrators are not always in accord with their viewpoint. Charges of insubordination are carefully examined by these dispute-settlers, who give considerable weight to extenuating factors and mitigating circumstances.

In the hundreds of cases researched for this section, no penalty whatsoever was permitted by arbitrators in 25 percent of the cases they evaluated.[72] This meant that some form of management punishment already imposed, from discharge to some lesser penalty, was disallowed and overturned. In another 40 percent of the cases researched, the arbitrator reduced the penalty to some lesser punishment in light of extenuating circumstances that had not been given sufficient consideration by the employer. In only 25 percent of the cases where discharge had been imposed by the company was this penalty upheld. In 10 percent of the cases a penalty less severe than discharge, as assessed by management, was upheld intact by the outside third party.

These figures demonstrate a very poor batting average by the management team in its arbitral efforts to have its previously taken position of demanding unquestioning obedience upheld. A careful reading of the cases where the company's decision was overruled reflects another factor. In many instances the agents of management were reacting emotionally and sometimes impulsively to employee challenges— questioning, criticism, interference, and the like—of company power and authority.

Insubordination seems to be the form of personal misconduct most often appearing in arbitration hearings. The majority of the cases researched apparently fall into two general categories.

One is the refusal or willful failure to obey orders as issued by representatives of management. The second category comprises cases where employees challenge, criticize, obstruct, abuse, or interfere with management's supervision in various ways. The second category generates the greatest number of lost or compromised arbitral decisions for management. Presuming that an order does not jeopardize the health, safety, or welfare of the employee, or require him to accede to an illegal or immoral demand, that it is reasonably within his capability, and that it does not cause him to lose some other contractual right or benefit, the majority of arbitrators will uphold the doctrine of "Obey first and grieve later." In any case, that appeared to be the supported premise when managements' action was upheld by the arbitrator in the cases constituting the first category.[73]

LOAFING

Loafing is dealt with here by itself as an issue separate from its companion issue of sleeping because it is often subjected to lesser penalties by arbitrators. Loafing may take many different forms. An employee may spend a lot of time talking with other employees; he may loiter in the rest room, in the vending machine area, or around the water cooler; he may wander from his machine or department into other sections where he does not belong. Whatever the kind of loafing, the result is that the worker is disengaged from his proper productive activity.

It is important in cases of this kind for management to establish that the employee is truly lingering and that his idleness is not legitimate or beyond his control. For example, a supervisor observed a group of employees clustered together and talking 55 minutes before the end of their shift. Disciplinary notices were issued to all these workers. Yet by his own admission, the foreman had actually watched them for no more than 30 seconds. He did not know how long they had been gathered together talking; nor did he inquire. He did not know whether they were discussing a production problem or the previous day's baseball game; nor did he ask them. He surmised that they might have stayed conversing aimlessly until the end of the shift, 55 minutes later. He assumed they were taking advantage of the absence of the foreman to quit work. In short, because he did not investigate the matter, his own testimony disabled the case that he postulated. The employees' grievance was sustained.[74]

Rules against loafing apply equally to union representatives and rank-and-file employees, as a union steward at the Caterpillar Tractor Company learned to his chagrin. The company imposed a three-day suspension on him for "poor work habits, consisting of excessive time away from the work area, wasting time at the machine, and visiting excessively," and specifically for spending an hour and 36 minutes away from his machine in one shift. The steward had received ample advance warning that he would be disciplined if he did not alter his conduct. In upholding the suspension, the arbiter commented in particular on one element of the case:

> One factor in this case that has given the Arbitrator pause in concluding that the Company had just cause for discipline is the concession that the Grievant was an average performer and produced 107% on the night of the events that caused the disciplinary layoff. One possible explanation of the apparent conflict of evidence between performance and excessive absence from the job is that average performance in general is at a somewhat low level. Another is the possibility that the Grievant worked at a much higher productive efficiency during the time spent on the job. In any event, however, in light of the overall record in this case, the Arbitrator believes that the performance level of the Grievant is not sufficient, either in degree or [in] import, to warrant negation of the rest of the record. For all the foregoing reasons, the grievance in this case cannot be supported.[75]

Discharges for Loafing

Although such cases are in the minority, discharges for a first offense of loafing have been upheld. An arbiter will sustain this penalty when he feels or actually is compelled by the language of the collective bargaining agreement to do so.

An example of this occurred in a dispute arising at the Bethlehem Steel Company. A worker was discharged for loafing on the job after the supervisor, who had searched for him for some time, found him sitting in a restricted area smoking a cigarette. The employee claimed he had been sent to the area by the supervisor, but this man denied the allegation. The arbiter sustained the discharge, commenting:

> The most damaging evidence against the Grievant is his admission that he was caught loafing. Irrespective of how much work he might have performed that evening by comparison with other members of the gang, the fact still remains that he deliberately abandoned his work in order to loaf. He has given as a reason for going to the forepeak area his instructions to obtain a piece of string. Again, the facts show that his Leaderman did not tell him to get any string in the forepeak area, which was an off-limit location. It is obvious X_____ went to this area to escape for a few minutes his work assignment. Finally, there is the matter of severity of penalty. In this case, there can be no question that under the circumstances the Company had a right to effect the discharge of X_____. Management could have found it desirable to be lenient and grant clemency to X_____ in the interest of generosity toward an unfortunate

employee who made a mistake. This was not the case. The Arbitrator has no authority within the nature of the grievance statement to propose now that Management grant clemency to this individual.[76]

The opposite finding was brought by Arbitrator Peter Di Leone in a dispute between the Indiana Desk Company, Inc. and the United Furniture Workers of America. The company discharged some employees who worked on the fourth floor of the plant but had been found shortly before noon waiting on the stairs near the first-floor time clock to punch out for lunch. Management had condoned this practice for many years. When it established a new rule prohibiting the practice, it communicated the change on a hit-or-miss basis. In the arbiter's view, moreover, the nature of the conduct involved suggested that a graduated system of punishment for violation of the rule was appropriate. He therefore reduced the discharges to one-week suspensions.[77]

This case brings home once again the points that rules must be reasonable, uniformly applied, and communicated properly to the employees they affect and that any punishment imposed for violations must fit the crime.

Arbitrator Samuel S. Kates ruled that the Martin Company was justified in discharging one engineer but not the other when both had left a boiler unattended to engage in conversation unrelated to their work. While they were talking in the office adjoining the boiler room, the coupling in the feed pump had broken, overheating the boiler. The arbiter held that the discharge penalty was too severe in the case of one of the men, who had had only two months on the job and who had behaved properly on discovering the situation by shutting off the burner and calling for his more experienced companion. Kates upheld the discharge of the other employee because this man had greater knowledge of the risk involved in leaving the boiler room unattended. In addition, he had lost his head on being summoned by the junior employee and pushed a button activating another pump, thereby sending water into the overheated boiler and causing $23,000 worth of damage.[78]

OVERTIME WORK REFUSED

The National Labor Relations Board has considered the refusal of a group of employees to work overtime as a form of "partial" strike that is an "unprotected" activity under the Labor Management Relations

Act,[79] and therefore, the employees cannot successfully ask the Board for reinstatement if they are discharged for their action.[80]

Under the provisions of labor agreements, it is well established that a company has the right to compel employees to work overtime in the absence of some contractual restriction.[81] It can compromise this general right if its insistence on the overtime is capricious or discriminatory, if its order to the employees has not been clearly and directly communicated, or if it has failed to take corrective steps in the face of previous refusals to work overtime.

Two of these points are illustrated by a dispute at Hussman, San Francisco (a Ray Winther Co. subsidiary), which imposed two-day disciplinary suspensions on 10 employees who refused to work emergency overtime. Arbiter James J. Willingham discovered that employees had consistently regarded unposted overtime as voluntary and had not been disciplined for previous refusals. Nor were they warned that they would be disciplined if they refused to work. Moreover, the evidence on whether the grievants were given a direct order to work overtime was conflicting and did not establish that they were. The arbiter therefore lifted the suspensions.[82]

Arbiter William Stix considered it an implicit obligation in a contract's grievance procedure for employees to accept the company's directives, even if disputed, and to grieve later. Therefore, a worker who rejected an overtime assignment was manifesting a do-it-yourself approach to a shop controversy that, like a collective work stoppage, constituted a direct challenge to the employer's authority.[83] Accordingly, the arbitrator upheld the company's two-day disciplinary layoff of employees who refused overtime work even though they believed that the assignment violated the contract.

Several arbiters have overruled discipline imposed on employees who declined to work on Christmas and New Year's Eve. As one opinion phrased it, these are "peculiar and sacred" holidays in our culture; therefore, the refusal to work on these overtime days is not a punishable offense since workers would suffer an irretrievable loss not recoverable under the concept of "work now, grieve later." [84]

Still other umpires have ruled that discipline was inappropriate where one or more of the following factors have been involved: (1) the amount of overtime required is excessively large; (2) the overtime work is not of the emergency type, and other workers are conveniently available; (3) no effort is made to obtain other employees more willing after those first assigned the work have declined; and (4) the overtime is announced so late that affected employees have insufficient time to adjust their personal schedules for transportation and other needs.[85]

PHYSICAL OR MENTAL DISABILITY

Arbitrators generally recognize management's right to discharge an employee who is physically unable to do the job, particularly if no other suitable positions are available. The case is often decided on the basis of medical testimony. The overwhelming majority of companies call on doctors they employ or select to make medical judgments of an employee's condition and his ability to perform his work. Arbiters generally uphold management's prerogative to rely on the opinion of its doctors, but they do consider that the employee has a right to introduce the conflicting opinion of his own medical adviser before the company's action becomes final.[86]

Most arbitrators are not medically trained, so that it is often extremely difficult for them to resolve differences between the conclusions of the company's and the employee's doctors. Management is usually well advised to attempt to reconcile such differences in advance of the arbitration proceedings. It might have the company doctor discuss the matter with the employee's doctor.[87] If this brings no reconciliation of opinion, the two physicians might jointly select a colleague to answer the questions between them and agree that the parties would be bound by his conclusions.

The dilemma of the arbitrator who must resolve differences of opinion between two, competent medical authorities was aptly expressed by Israel Ben Scheiber:

> Just as in the words of the inimitable Gilbert and Sullivan, a policeman's lot is not a happy one, so too, a layman who is called on to decide sharply conflicting testimony by members of the medical profession is placed in a most unhappy situation, especially where the potentials of his decision may be a serious impact on the parties who depend on his good judgment.[88]

A review of a large number of awards involving discharge because of physical disability shows that the most material issue to arbitrators is whether the company's action has been arbitrary, capricious, or unreasonable. In an Alcoa dispute, nationally known Arbitrator Paul Prasow stated the principle as follows: "It can be said, then, that the Company's obligation was to act in a fair and reasonable manner, without discrimination, and with due regard for the welfare of the employee as well as for the requirements of efficient and even operation. Now, has the Company acted in a fair and reasonable manner in this situation?"[89]

This question arose in a grievance against Atlas Chemical Industries, Inc. by the International Chemical Workers Union. Arbitrator LeRoy Autrey concluded that the company had not acted arbitrarily or unreasonably in discharging an employee suffering from pulmonary difficulties. Despite a conflict in specific medical findings, five doctors recommended that he not be allowed to work in a dusty atmosphere, and no contrary medical judgment was advanced. The evidence indicated that he was not qualified for any job with the company other than as a truck driver, which exposed him to considerable lignite dust.[90]

An employee's own doctor's conclusions can lead to his discharge. At the Goss Company, a man submitted a claim for disability benefits under the employer's insurance program, accompanying it by a statement from his own physician that he was permanently disabled. The company thereupon terminated his employment. The union argued that the employer was obliged to seek other medical opinion, and at the arbitration hearing, which came three months after the discharge, it submitted another doctor's statement that the employee was capable of performing full-time work. Arbitrator Albert A. Epstein upheld the termination on the grounds that the procedure followed by the employee was of his own choosing and that the new medical opinion was not relevant to the situation existing at the time of his discharge.[91]

Arbitrator Claire V. Duff was called on to render a decision in a case involving an employee whose eyesight had deteriorated to a point below the accepted minimum level for his industry. He held that the employee was permanently disabled and that his discharge was proper.[92]

The same arbiter decided a dispute between the Kurtz Brothers, Inc. and the Clearfield Pressmen and Printing Workers Union. An allergy prevented an employee from working in an industrial environment where certain substances such as printer's ink were present. The allergy persisted for many years, and it appeared to be a permanent disability as far as work at this plant was concerned. Arbitrator Duff ruled that the company had proper cause for discharging the employee.[93]

Some chronic conditions, however, are not viewed as a bar to continued employment even though they seem severe. For example, epilepsy in and of itself has generally not been considered cause for discharge. In several disputes that involved the employment of epileptics, arbitrators have held against discharge where there was no compelling evidence of any safety hazard attendant on the affliction.[94]

Cases involving mental illness are difficult to categorize. Most employers hesitate to reemploy a person who has suffered a mental illness.

This is particularly so where the fear exists that it may recur. Despite their recognition of this, arbitrators have refused to uphold discharges where there was medical evidence that the employee had recovered at least to the extent that his return to work would not constitute an undue risk.[95]

Immoral conduct may be caused by mental illness. In disputes involving discharge for this reason, arbitrators have directed reinstatement when evidence has been provided that the illness has been cured. However, such awards have been based in part on the fact that the employee's fellow workers had no objection to his reinstatement.[96]

The question of narcotics addiction, which has both physical and mental effects, has aroused increasing concern in the industrial community as in society at large during recent years. One arbitrator, looking to the rapid deterioration caused by drug abuse, held the Chicago Pneumatic Tool Company to be justified in having discharged an employee who pleaded guilty to charges of obtaining narcotics through fraud and deceit and who was found to be addicted to cocaine. The arbiter reasoned that the addict's state, though the result of off-duty conduct, affected the employment relationship in that his degeneration could at any time reach the point where it would seriously endanger the health and safety of fellow employees and company equipment.[97]

RETIREMENT AGE

It seems to be a well-established principle that layoffs, discharges, and retirement are "completely different" methods of terminating employment.[98] Accordingly, it is commonly held that contract provisions relating to layoffs and discharges have no relevance to disputes involving compulsory retirement for age.

Labor agreements often accord special transfer prerogatives to the handicapped and aged in connections other than with retirement or pensions. Twenty-nine percent of agreements in 1969 contained some arrangement for handling handicapped workers and 12 percent mentioned aged employees. The majority of these contracts granted preference or consideration for any lighter work available to employees who had given long and faithful service and could no longer handle their duties.

Employers appear to be able to establish compulsory retirement dates unilaterally where the union has acquiesced in this action. An example is found in a case involving the Hercules Powder Co. Despite the union's claim that it had never agreed to compulsory retirement, an arbiter upheld the company's right to retire an employee who had reached the age set forth in a unilaterally established plan. The plan had been in effect for five years, and numerous employees had been retired under it without objection from the union. Also significant was the absence of any contractual provision barring compulsory retirement.[99]

The arbiter in another case went even farther. He held that General Aniline & Film Corp. (now GAF Corporation) could unilaterally establish a compulsory retirement age for its employees provided the contract was silent on the subject and the company could demonstrate that such a policy was not unreasonable, arbitrary, or discriminatory.[100]

SAFETY

Employers generally recognize their obligation to provide a safe and healthful working place for their employees. The degree to which they fulfill this requirement varies. Regrettably, there are companies that do not give so much attention to this aspect of their business as they do to such matters as production, quality, and schedules. Too many seem to feel that this responsibility can always be deferred to another time, and too often that time comes only when complaints or accidents rise critically or the current disposable income of the business is large.

Many employers, on the other hand, consistently consider the health and safety of their workers among their highest priorities. Again regrettably, not enough credit is given these firms for their commendable commitment. Their reasons are both practical and humane. The factor of practicality relates to such considerations as insurance premium costs, workmen's compensation expenses, and reputation in the manpower marketplace. The humane factor speaks for itself.

Safety, health, and sanitary conditions are naturally always of concern to any labor organization that represents the employer's workers. In addition, there are various municipal, state, and federal laws and regulations that most employers must operate within. It is therefore quite common for a labor agreement to contain some form of pledge from the company that it will give attention to these aspects of working conditions. A few examples of such contract clauses provide a sampling of their variety.

One provision states the employer's intention to conform with any applicable statutes or regulations: "The Management agrees to provide and maintain proper safety and sanitary devices throughout its plants, in accordance with Federal, State and local standards." [101] Another contract reads: "The Employer agrees to comply with all standards of sanitation provided by the New Jersey State laws. The Employer agrees to conduct fire drills in accordance with the requirement of the New Jersey State law." [102]

Frequently found are provisions that explicitly specify the company's responsibilities concerning the health and safety of its employees. These clauses are common even when the employer is not embraced by government regulations, which means that he is voluntarily accepting the obligation. The following are examples:

> The company will make provisions for the safety and health of the employees during the hours of their employment. Protective devices and other equipment necessary to protect the employees from injury, or safeguard their health, will be provided by the Company and all employees will abide by the safety rules and regulations. The Company will have a nurse in attendance in the First Aid Hospital at all times when there are any employees working in the plant.[103]

> The Company will make adequate provisions for the safety and health of the employees, and will supply special safety equipment necessary to properly protect employees from injury without cost to the employee where the necessity for such equipment is agreed upon by the Company and the Union.[104]

It goes without saying that neither the inclusion of provisions like these nor the employer's utmost efforts will alone insure a safe and healthful working place. A great part of the responsibility for achieving this end rests with the employee and the union, whose cooperation is expressly solicited in some contracts. Unsafe and unwise acts committed by workers can produce accidents, even disaster, in the safest environment. Unfortunately, it is sometimes necessary for management to exercise its disciplinary authority to bring this point to its workers.

In contrast, employees sometimes refuse to perform work because, they contend, it will jeopardize their own or other workers' safety, health, or welfare. The refusal may actually be well founded: there may be a genuine risk present that can be demonstrated. But at best, the worker who raises such an objection is treading on uncertain ground.

The delicate nature of this question is evidenced in a dispute at the Wilcolator Co., where a walkout occurred over a presumed health hazard. Arbiter James V. Altieri concluded that the employees' belief, though sincere, was not sufficient justification for the walkout, for they had not established that the hazard did in fact exist.[105]

Arbitrator Marlin Volz sustained the suspension by the Metal Specialty Products Corp. of eight employees who walked off their jobs to attend a union meeting regarding a dispute over the safety of plant machinery. The contract contained specific provisions for handling these questions of which the workers and union officials should have been aware.[106]

Arbitral Principles

Each case brought to arbitration that concerns an employee's accident record is judged on its individual merits, as are disputes based on all other issues. But it is possible to encapsulate general concepts that influence arbitral conclusions.

The majority of arbitrators look askance at a management's contention that a discharge has been imposed because an employee is "accident prone." The comments of Arbiter Alexander H. Frey summarize the attitude in the profession toward such a claim:

. . . industrial discipline, especially the supreme penalty of discharge, should not be based upon the conclusion that a given employee is "accident prone." Without having been careless or negligent, a driver may be involved in a series of accidents for which he is blameless; if so, there is no basis for punishment. A driver may drive illegally or recklessly and luckily escape accidents for a period of time; such a driver merits discipline. . . .[107]

When an employee is discharged because of his accident record, the requirement of just cause makes it incumbent upon the company to prove that he was culpably careless or negligent, not merely an involved party. Another factor is the seriousness of the accident that results in discharge. If worse incidents have been excused or given lesser disciplinary penalties, discharge will generally be considered too severe for a subsequent accident of smaller consequence.

In the dispute decided by Arbiter Frey, both these factors are revealed. A truck driver for the Interstate Bakeries Corporation was discharged after his fourth accident. Two previous ones had not been his fault; a serious one that was attributable to his negligence had brought him a suspension. The fourth accident, nearly nine months later, was relatively minor and did not clearly involve negligence on his part.

Given these particulars, the arbitrator viewed the discharge as "manifestly unfair" and reinstated the driver without loss of seniority and with back pay to the date of his discharge minus four weeks.

Just as involvement in an accident would not establish an employee's responsibility for it and thus justify his discharge, nor would cancellation of the company's insurance coverage or a substantial increase in its premiums. This was the issue in a dispute over the discharge of a truck driver three weeks after he had been involved in an accident. During the three-week period, he had continued to work and carry out driving assignments. The company discharged him the same day it received a letter from its insurance carrier asserting that the employee had been negligent and threatening the cancellation of its coverage if he was not fired. In the arbitration hearing, management offered no evidence that the grievant had been at fault in any way—neither it nor the insurance company had made any investigation of the accident—but claimed it had an established policy of dismissing any driver who had an accident, regardless of fault. The arbitrator commented, "We need not pass on the propriety of such a rule, when the evidence made clear that discharges were not triggered by accidents but by letters from the insurance company. Indeed, this is evident from the fact that the grievant was allowed to continue driving for nearly three weeks after the accident, but was discharged immediately when the letter arrived." [108]

Some Special Issues

A case involving the McLouth Steel Corp. contained two elements that constituted problems to the arbitrator in reaching his conclusions: the employee's accident record and the fact that the company had demoted the offender rather than disciplining or discharging him. The employee, a crane operator, had three safety incidents in the space of 16 months. The first was apparently of a kind that is not uncommon. The second was more serious in that the grievant ignored or was unaware of the danger to which he subjected a fellow employee. The third was the most serious because it highlighted his apparent inability to take into account factors that are fundamental in operating a crane safely. A welder was repairing a furnace roof in the area where the crane was working, and though he was out of sight under the roof, a red light signaled his presence. Despite this, the grievant attempted to set down the crane bucket, which was about 10 feet in diameter and 13 feet high. It struck the roof, dislodging some of the roof bricks. The worker's welding shield was pinned by the bricks and broken, but he slipped out of the hood and fell to the floor, escaping injury. This incident brought about the crane operator's demotion to general labor.

After considering these circumstances and with the safety of all the workers in mind, the arbitrator did not believe he should reverse the action of the company officials directly responsible for and intimately acquainted with the day-to-day operations of the plant. After all, the best evidence of a safe operator is the absence of accidents.[109]

The next case is interesting for the reason that an employee's failure to report accidents was as instrumental in his discharge as were the accidents themselves. The employer, the Thiokol Chemical Corporation, operated a government plant producing a critical product, which made strict adherence to rules a necessity. The grievant was discharged following the last of three incidents, none of which endangered lives directly or cost great sums of money but none of which he reported to the supervisor, as well-known company regulations required. He had been suspended for the same failure on two prior occasions. With the third offense—neglecting to report that he had installed the wrong structural steel beam in a plant building— he was discharged.

Arbitrator Marion Beatty remarked, ". . . it is the employee's refusal to report such incidents that I believe justifies the Company's deciding this employee is not a safe and proper person to have on its premises." The grievance was denied.[110]

A large number of arbitration cases over the issue of safety involve company truck drivers. The dangers of operating a vehicle are obvious from the national statistics on injuries, deaths, and property losses from road and highway accidents. In fact, trucking concerns, recognizing this occupational hazard, commonly adopt contractual provisions that express particular concern about driving safety.

Arbitrators show this same concern by their reluctance to disturb disciplinary discharges for accidents where it means returning an employee to the highway who may be dangerous or where the company's legal and financial welfare is at stake.[111] Within this framework, arbiters have generally upheld discharges of drivers who have had numerous accidents and/or a poor past record, as in the following cases:

1. Four accidents in 10 months and a driving record significantly worse than other drivers' (Standard Oil Company of California).[112]
2. Six accidents in three years (Ward Baking Company).[113]

3. Five accidents within one year (Chevy Chase Dairy).[114]
4. An extremely bad past record and one serious accident (Hudson County Bus Owners Assoc.).[115]
5. A serious pattern of speeding that caused a third accident (Schreiver Company Trucking).[116]
6. Seven accidents in five years with a persistently deteriorating accident record (Kroger Company).[117]

On the other hand, the penalty of discharge has been set aside and reinstatement ordered (usually without back pay) under the following circumstances:

1. Negligence not conclusively shown for a second accident in six months, which the arbiter saw as the result of a "moment of inadvertence" and not "willful misconduct or gross negligence" (Safe Bus Company, Inc.).[118]
2. No danger to the public (Safe Bus Company, Inc.).[119]
3. Ordinary negligence, as distinguished from gross negligence or willful or wanton conduct (American Synthetic Rubber Corp.).[120]

SLEEPING

Proving an employee was sleeping is a most difficult task. The excuses offered are a tribute to human inventiveness. They range from praying to meditating (with closed eyes) on the sterling attributes of the supervisor who has caught the sleeper in the act.

Because they recognize the complications of proving a worker was sleeping, many managers choose instead to call the offense "neglect of duty," "inattention to appointed tasks with resulting hazards to safety," or some other locution appropriate to the circumstances. If there is evidence that the worker was in such a relaxed or supine physical state that he was not fulfilling his responsibilities, an arbitrator will usually not require that actual sleeping be proved.

Whatever the charge, it is always beneficial to the company's case if the employee's behavior has been witnessed by more than one person. It may be able to prove he was indeed asleep if witnesses can testify that they woke him or stood beside him until he awoke.[121] They may reasonably conclude that he is sleeping, said Arbitrator Carl A. Warns in a Lockheed Aircraft Corp. case, when he is in repose with this eyes closed and is unresponsive during several minutes of close observation.[122]

An employee's disciplinary record and length of service are frequently taken into consideration in grievance hearings on this issue. Arbitrators seem inclined to reduce discharges to suspensions without pay when the offending employee has a combination of a clear work history and several years of good and faithful service. This is particularly true when it is the worker's first offense.

The nature of the employee's job also has a bearing on the arbitral conclusions. For example, sleeping while on duty is a more serious matter for a plant guard than a materials clerk. Therefore, arbiters would be more likely to uphold a discharge for the guard's first offense than the clerk's, and would do so even if the guard had an exceptionally good personal record.

Where an established rule or practice regarding sleeping has been consistently and uniformly applied to erring workers and where the penalty has been discharge, arbiters will generally uphold that action as proper.[123] They will do so as well even if no specific rule is in force if the offense involves some danger to the safety of employees or a hazard to equipment.[124]

THEFT

There is little question that stealing constitutes an offense warranting discharge and is consequently one of the gravest acts of which an employee may be accused or found guilty. In fact, it is so serious that rarely does any specific warning precede a discharge decision.[125]

Challenging the fairness or propriety of a rule against stealing is an exercise in futility for a union. Arbitral reaction to such an attempt is best summed up in a decision brought down by Arbitrator Paul Lehoczky:

> Rules that represent simple translations of the laws (common or statute) which set up the public code of conduct (physical violence, destruction, immoral acts, etc., and including theft) cannot be ruled as "unfair" as compared to rules dealing with smoking, garnishment of wages and the like, peculiar to the operation of the enterprise in question.[126]

Unlike misconduct that relates uniquely to the working place, such as absenteeism, loafing, and insubordination, stealing is also reprehensible in the whole of society. The person who takes a job brings with him the prior knowledge that stealing is a crime against society and that it is equally a crime against his employer.

Because of the gravity of this offense and its threat to the name and reputation of one found guilty of it, arbitrators impose a heavy burden of proof on the accusing party. It is probably for this reason also that they overturn a large majority of discharges for theft. Practitioners disagree on the quantum of proof that is required of an employer, but most would likely concur that a higher degree of proof than the "preponderance of the evidence," which is the approach used most frequently in arbitration proceedings, is usually required when the alleged misconduct is of a kind recognized and punished by the criminal law.[127]

The reluctance of arbiters to uphold discharge actions for stealing unless the evidence is compelling is understandable. The person found guilty not only loses his job with his present employer but may very well be stigmatized in the eyes of the entire industrial community within his locale, and the public knowledge of his prosecution may bring social injury to his family. Arbiters cannot be faulted for proceeding with concern and caution.

Reviewing the rulings in a few cases will highlight how arbitrators treat the question of sufficient proof.

In a dispute at the Great Atlantic & Pacific Tea Co., Inc., Arbiter Marlin Volz held that the company did not have just cause for discharging an employee who was seen emerging from a meat cooler with a package of dried beef in his hand and who failed to offer an immediate explanation. The worker made no effort to conceal the package, and the story he subsequently provided for why he had the package remained consistent when he retold it. His record was good and clean and contained no prior charge of pilferage. The arbiter ruled that the evidence did not establish guilt of theft clearly and convincingly. However, he did believe that the worker was guilty of unauthorized possession of company property, for which a two-week suspension without pay would be an appropriate penalty.[128]

Arbitrator Burton B. Turkus supported the discharge of an employee by the United Parcel Service, Inc. on the basis of independent, clear, and convincing evidence that the man had participated in the theft of $200,000 in money orders. His refusal to testify was a proper exercise of his constitutional protection against self-incrimination, particularly since criminal proceedings against him were then pending, and no implication of guilt or innocence was attached to his silence. But that privilege did not guarantee him reinstatement in his job when independent evidence of his dishonesty established his guilt.[129]

Chapter 5

Reasons for Discipline or Discharge: Off-Duty Activities

The majority of offenses that would bring down discipline were they to occur on the job are not subject to company action if they happen off the job, off company premises, and during nonworking time. Generally the employer is not entitled to take issue with a worker's off-duty behavior, for this would constitute invasion of his privacy and curtailment of his freedom of action. However, certain kinds of conduct may be construed as so closely related to job activities or relationships that they compel management's attention, and arbiters have upheld employers who have disciplined workers found guilty of them.

In an opinion on a conflict-of-interest case to be discussed in the following section, the arbitrator summarized and illustrated this concept:

> While it is true as a general proposition that an Employer may not regulate an employee's personal activities while away from the plant, this rule has several exceptions and qualifications. The converse of the rule is that an employee may not engage in activities on his own time, and while away from the plant, which are reasonably calculated to adversely affect the employer's interest. The application of these principles is necessarily dependent upon the nature of the employment and the circumstances in each individual case. By way of illustration, it would be highly doubtful that an employer could promulgate a rule forbidding

112

off-duty consumption of alcoholic beverages. However, an employee could be subject to discipline when he reports for work under the influence of alcohol, and where his condition interferes with his work performance and endangers the safety of fellow employees. Generally, an employee may engage in outside activities unrelated to his employment; however, it is questionable that the employee could properly expend time and energy on unrelated projects to the extent that he would become fatigued and physically and mentally incapable of performing his job. In such instances, the conduct of the employee outside of the plant would directly affect his job performance and would be the legitimate concern of management.[1]

Off-duty activities that have been considered to be eligible for company discipline include the following:

1. Behavior that harms the company's reputation or product.[2]
2. Pursuit of a job feud outside the plant with a very real risk of a renewal of the feud back on the job,[3] or assault that clearly arises out of the working relationship between the employees and not out of personal differences.[4]
3. Conduct that makes other employees reluctant or unable to work with the offender.[5]
4. Conduct that evinces a dangerous propensity, a criminal tendency, or serious emotional instability in the employee and that is likely to manifest itself on the job.[6]
5. Off-duty behavior that shows the employee to be a bad industrial risk.[7]
6. Conditions that impair the efficiency or attendance of the worker, such as alcoholism.[8]

COMPETITION WITH THE EMPLOYER

While resolving a dispute between Radio Buffalo, Inc. and the National Association of Broadcast Employees and Technicians, Arbitrator Peter Seitz made the following observations:

The relationship of employer and employee is one of mutual trust and confidence. An employer, in consideration of [the] duties and obligations which he owes to the employee, is entitled to the assurance that the employee will not engage in interests damaging to the enterprise. The good faith that is implicit in and is an inarticulate premise of every contract guarantees that. Such an assurance does not need expression in the contract. In its absence it is reasonable and proper for an employer to promulgate a rule or regulation prohibiting "conflict of interest" activities. Lacking any general rule, an employer may find other appropriate means of bringing it home to an employee that his outside activities on behalf of a competing employer are detrimental to the enterprise and inconsistent with his duties as an employee.[9]

Thus, even when no written instrument expresses it, a principle underlying the employment relationship is that a worker will not conduct himself in a manner detrimental to the interests of his employer. Most companies assume that each employee will engage only in activities that will promote the welfare of the organization supporting him. After all, his livelihood is derived from that relationship, and it is ill advised to bite the hand that feeds one.

Sometimes employers promulgate rules that forbid outside activities such as moonlighting, an offense that will be treated separately later in this chapter. Or the rules may state that employees will be subject to discipline if they commit acts of disloyalty or engage in pursuits that compete with the employer's operations. When a company believes a worker is doing something that is a real or potential threat to its interests, it attempts to curtail this by punishing the offender.

The reasonableness of such rules is often in contention and is usually determined on the basis of how broad their scope is. Arbiters tend to look askance at rules that appear to maintain an arbitrary control over employees after work. But where a rule is specifically limited in its application to the performance of similar outside work, it is generally viewed as having been designed explicitly and uniquely to maintain the well-being of the company. This has been the holding where such rules have been challenged by the union.[10]

Several factors usually have a bearing on the outcome of a dispute over an allegation of competitive work. Most of these are common to other types of disciplinary issues, such as whether a rule existed, whether it was generally made known to the employees, and whether it was uniformly and regularly applied. Some questions are peculiar to this issue: Was the action of the offender a real or only a potential threat to the company? Did the company in fact experience some injury?

A number of these factors influenced the arbitrator's decision in a case involving the New York Central Railroad Company (now Penn Central Transportation Company). A yardman it employed also practiced law on the side. For several years, he had acted as attorney for fellow employees in prosecuting claims for personal injury damages against the carrier. He had done this with the company's knowledge, but ultimately it became offended at the practice and discharged him. However, there was no specific rule covering activities like his, and there was no evidence that in its absence any prior warning had been issued to him. Arbitrator Hubert Wyckoff commented:

> There is ancient authority for the proposition that a man cannot serve two masters; and as a lawyer the Claimant must have been fully aware of this principle. . . .

> There is no rule in this Labor Agreement, and the Carrier has not issued a specific rule, that will support the charge made here. This is not necessarily fatal, for there are certain types of conduct such as murdering passengers or wrecking trains that could hardly be condoned for the want of a rule.

> The difficulty with this case is that, with the Carrier's knowledge, Claimant has previously engaged in the conduct for which he is now dismissed without any charge ever before having been lodged against him by the Carrier. Whatever may have been the Carrier's reasons for not charging him in the prior cases, in the absence of a specific rule, Claimant was at least entitled to a warning; and there is no evidence that he ever received one.[11]

Thus holding, the arbitrator ordered the reinstatement of the worker but without payment for time lost. This certainly put the employee on notice. He now had been warned. If he practiced law again, it would surely lead to his permanent dismissal.

Proof of Actual Loss

There is some disagreement over whether the employer must establish that the business was indeed harmed by the worker's outside activities. Arbitrator John E. Gorsuch is one expert who has subscribed to the philosophy that there need be no direct demonstration of actual damage to the principal employer since the very situation itself is injurious to him.[12]

The arbitrator in the following matter was from the same school. A company that fabricated various types of aluminum bodies for trucks discharged an employee for assisting his brother in a small aluminum welding business that also included the building of aluminum truck bodies. At the arbitration hearing, the company stated that it had lost work valued at $9,000 to $12,000 in a three-month period as a result of the competition from this concern. The shop rules contained a rule that engaging in business competitive with the company's products would be considered cause for discharge. The company pointed to the likelihood that association by its employees with competitors would give those firms access to valuable information regarding design and production techniques, including engineering and experimental work developed by it at considerable expense and effort, and that this could enable the competitors to undercut its established prices. It also expressed the fear that knowledge gained at its plant might be used for contacting customers in order to obtain orders, a fear enhanced by the fact that such information was readily available to employees in the grievant's classification.

The arbiter made some highly lucid observations that indicate the prevailing arbitral opinion on this issue:

> It is a well-recognized principle in industrial relations that an employee should not engage in outside employment which suggests a conflict of interest and divided loyalty. It would be manifestly unfair for an employee to work for an Employer during the day and for a competitor evenings, particularly where the work performed for the latter could reasonably involve the use of technical information, skills, and techniques acquired as a result of the employment relationship. To do so would constitute a situation of indirect competition between the employee and his employer, and would be violative of the implied conditions of employment which are inherent in the relationship. . . .

> In situations involving conflict of interests, it is not necessarily required that the Employer convincingly establish that a business detriment or financial loss has in fact resulted; it is sufficient if the off-duty relationship is such as would reasonably suggest that the outside employment would lead to a disclosure to the competitor of information and skills acquired by the employee, and this is particularly true when the competing employer is engaged in a similar type of business and in the same general geographical area. The situation would tend to destroy the element of confidence which an employer must have, and would inhibit the disclosure of production information, engineering skills, and procedures. Information acquired through the ingenuity, research, and financial expenditures of an employer should not be siphoned off through the back door by employees whose loyalties are divided between their employer and its competitors.[13]

It was the conclusion of this chairman that the enterprise for which the grievant worked part time was in direct competition with the employer and that this gave rise to a conflict of interest. The discharge was sustained.

This was not a case of mere moonlighting, which is distinguishable. Rules against moonlighting are mainly concerned with the division of an employee's energies between two employers. The situation considered above was an intolerable one for the employer and constituted a breach of an implied condition of employment as well as of a plant rule.

In another case, the employer was adjudged to have improperly discharged an employee for disloyalty. Without stating the point explicitly, this arbiter implied that he also needed proof of some real detriment or loss to the company. The offending employee had visited the plant of a competitor during his vacation and corresponded with its president both before and after the visit. Later he refused to divulge to his company's attorney any information he had gained from these contacts about its patent infringement suit against the competitor. Although the arbiter viewed the employee's action as tactless and potentially injurious to the employer, there was no direct evidence that he caused or intended to cause harm or that his actions were illegal. Moreover, it was material to the arbitrator that the employee engaged in this activity while on his own time.[14]

CRIMINAL RECORD

Some employers—probably a majority—consider a job applicant with a criminal record as undesirable or at least of questionable character for employment. Rightly or wrongly, fairly or unfairly, they are unwilling to forgive and forget.

It is one thing to have such a policy as a preemployment factor; unsuccessful applicants have few means of challenging their rejection. It is quite another to adopt this viewpoint regarding members of the workforce in good standing who are convicted of illegal acts; there is a labor organization to represent their interests, and there are arbitrators to pass judgment on management's disciplinary action.

Arbiters appear to apply certain general concepts in cases of discharge for illegal or immoral conduct. If an employee has no previous criminal record, has worked for the company for some time satisfactorily, and has engaged in the improper activity outside of working hours and off company premises, his dismissal will probably not be sustained as long as his offense does not injure his effectiveness on the job or damage his company's reputation in the marketplace or in the industrial community. If one or more of the contrary conditions are present, the discharge is more likely to be upheld. In sustaining a discharge in a dispute between the Chicago Pneumatic Tool Company and the International Association of Machinists, Arbiter Clair V. Duff stated the basic operative principle in these words:

> Arbitrators are reluctant to sustain discharges based on off-duty conduct of employees unless a direct relationship between off-duty conduct and employment is proved. Discretion must be exercised lest employers become censors of community morals. However, where socially reprehensible conduct and employment duties and risks are substantially related, conviction for certain types of crimes may justify discharge.[15]

Discipline for Illegal Activities

An employee of the Babcock & Wilcox Company was indicted on the charge of contributing to the delinquency of a minor, which is a misdemeanor under Pennsylvania law. He subsequently pleaded guilty and was sentenced to imprisonment for six months. Midway in its term, he was released and placed on parole for the remainder of his sentence. While in jail, he was notified by the company that he was discharged. His prior record as an employee was good, and the incident occurred off plant premises and outside of working hours. The union grieved and the matter was arbitrated. The pertinent comments of Arbitrator Duff are as follows:

> Even if Grievant's conduct is viewed in its most undesirable light, there is no relationship between the offense and Grievant's status as an employee. Grievant did not tend to corrupt the morals of any employee. . . . There is no reason why any fellow employee would have any reluctance to continue working with Grievant. The Plant Rule which prohibits "Conduct which violates the common decency or morality of the community" is reasonable and enforceable so long as it is applied to conduct which directly relates to the employer-employee relationship. This Rule cannot authorize the Company to punish off-duty conduct of employees who violate the criminal code of the Commonwealth, unless such infractions are related to the business of the Company. The evidence fails to prove any relationship between this unsavory incident in Grievant's private life and his usefulness as an employee. . . .[16]

It is clear that this was a situation where the employee's improper behavior while functioning in society on his own time did not have any impact on the employer-employee relationship. Arbitrator Duff reinstated him in his former position without back pay.

As a testimony to consistency, the same arbitrator reaffirmed the pertinent concept and upheld a discharge in a case involving Robertshaw Controls Company and the Steelworkers union. The reprehensible conduct was sexual perversion with young boys of the community, and the facts indicated that a discernible relationship did exist between the criminal acts and the status of the grievant as an employee.[17]

A worker had been employed by the New Haven Gas Company for approximately seven years. He was charged with embezzlement in connection with his part-time employment by a laundromat. After pleading guilty, he was given a six-month suspended sentence and placed on probation for two years. As a result of the conviction, he was discharged by the gas company. In support of its action, the company pointed out that it was a public utility and as such was expected by its customers to maintain higher standards among its employees than other enterprises whose position did not directly affect the public interest. It had in its possession 3,500 keys to customers' premises for use by meter readers and service men in the event no one was at home. Although the grievant did not have either of these positions, the labor agreement did permit him to exercise his seniority to take one of the jobs if he was qualified to perform it.

The union argued that the crime had nothing to do with the employee's work for the gas company. He lost no time from work as a result of his arrest and conviction. The utility was acting as if it owned an employee for 24 hours a day.

In the arbitrator's view, the overriding consideration was the public nature of the company's business and the position of trust its personnel must maintain with the public. The public was not aware that the grievant did not have access to customers' homes or keys. Moreover, he could transfer to one of the jobs that would make the keys available to him. In view of these factors and the nature of the employee's crime, the arbiter ruled that the company had proper cause to discharge him.[18]

A dairy was held to be justified in having suspended a route salesman charged with pandering and obscene exhibition even though the arrest occurred while he was on vacation and the contract did not impose off-duty ethical or moral standards on members of the unit. This was the ruling of Arbiter Charles L. Mullin, Jr., who expressed the opinion that insofar as management bears responsibility for meeting competition and maintaining goodwill, it alone is to estimate the possibility of an employee's continuing to perform as a salesman. The fact that the name of the dairy and the man's occupational identity were withheld in newspaper accounts was not significant. The arrest was publicized in the relatively small town where he lived and where his route was located. Thus he would inescapably be recognized by his name and identified by his customers in his capacity as one of the dairy's salesmen.[19]

Discipline for Absences Necessitated by Jail Sentences

Ordinarily, an employee has the duty to report for work when scheduled. In the Pennsylvania case discussed earlier, the employee who was convicted of contributing to the delinquency of a minor was of course absent from work during his time in jail. Although this was his own fault, it was not of itself a sufficiently grave offense to provide just cause for discharge under the contract, particularly since he had no history of unwarranted absenteeism. As Arbitrator Duff remarked, "There must be a reasonable proportionality between an offense and the penalty of discharge." The union had prudently not asked for back wages.[20]

A 37-year unblemished work record was the salvation of the employee in the next case. The worker was arrested on a morals charge at a motion picture theater. After serving a nine-month jail sentence, he went to the plant and attempted to return to his job. He was told that he was discharged. The contract recognized the right of the company to discipline an employee who absented himself from work without just cause. The arbiter found that proper cause for discharge did not exist. The worker's long and clean work record was the major factor weighing in his favor after three other circumstances were taken into account. First, the nature of the offense did not impair his ability to perform his job functions. Second, the underlying psychiatric problem that led to the offense did not in itself render him unfit for further employment, and there was no suggestion that the problem had not been cured or at least significantly improved by treatment. Third, his nine-month absence had no demonstrable adverse effect on operations, and it cost the employer nothing.[21]

An employee with 16 years' service who had always been considered a good worker and a good employee was arrested for allegedly having taken indecent liberties with a nine-year-old girl. The grievant pleaded guilty to the charge. The company then dropped him from employment on the ground that he had been off five days without reporting for scheduled work and was a quit. The arbiter did not agree, for the employee's wife had promptly notified the company at the time of his arrest and newspaper accounts of the incident had come to the company's attention. The worker did not intend to quit and had not "absented himself" from work within the meaning of the contract since that provision did not apply to involuntary absences. The fact that the grievant had been a factory worker tended to minimize any adverse effect on the morale or efficiency of other employees, and he was not in contact with the public in any way. The arbiter held the discharge as improper.[22]

FEUDING

It should be treated as a valid proposition that discipline may rightly be imposed when an incident occurring off company property has its roots at the plant and is clearly related or prejudicial to working conditions in the factory. Such is the case with fights or attacks generated by a feud between two or more employees.

An employee of the United States Steel Corporation went to his supervisor's home, complained of a remark the supervisor had made at work, and struck him on the head with a blunt instrument. Although the assault occurred away from the plant and outside of working hours, Arbitrator Sylvester Garrett upheld the discharge of the employee since the dispute stemmed directly from the working relationship in the plant. In so doing, he remarked, "While public authority also is available to deal with those who willfully commit assault and battery, this does not deprive Management of essential authority to maintain discipline and to protect members of supervision from unprovoked reprisals by dissatisfied employees away from work." [23]

The late Harry Shulman, who was permanent arbitrator for Ford Motor Company and the UAW, once pointed out, ". . . the jurisdictional line which limits the company's power of discipline is a functional, not a physical line" and is concerned with the "proximity of the relationship between the conduct and the employment." [24]

There are arbitration precedents for the contention that an employee on his own time and off company property is subject only to the restraints of civil law and not to the authority of the employer.[25] Despite these findings, the established principle is that the employer does have the right to discipline employees for off-duty altercations that are work-related and that are not simply the result of a mutual agreement to settle a matter outside of working hours in the ancient if no longer honorable method of recourse to fists.[26]

Sometimes a dispute that raises the issue of off-duty misconduct will involve an offense committed on company premises. At the Inland Container Corporation, an employee who had a long-standing feud with a fellow worker entered the plant intoxicated one day when he was off duty and threatened the other man with a gun. He refused to leave the premises and was finally taken off by the foreman. The employer discharged him. The union argued that the company should have depended on civil authorities to discipline him. Arbitrator D. Emmett Ferguson upheld the company's action on the ground that it could discharge even an off-duty worker if his wrongful acts injured the business. A man's right to personal liberty did not extend to the point of allowing him to invade company property and threaten a fellow employee.[27]

GARNISHMENTS

Management's enforcement of garnishment rules is an area where there is no uniformity of thinking among arbitrators. One of the factors producing this condition is that garnishments result from an employee's off-duty behavior.

Despite the complications they typically experience before arbitrators, companies persist in attempting to enforce garnishment rules. They probably do so in an effort to prevent employees from involving them in an endless series of wage levies. Garnishments are troublesome and expensive for a company to administer. They engage the time and efforts of supervisors and clerical employees and may even take other personnel away from their work for court appearances and the like.

The problems surrounding garnishment, coupled with the fact that this is a societal issue, are sufficiently large to have moved the federal government to enact legislation on it: Title III of the Consumer Credit Protection Act, which became effective July 1, 1970. This law restricts the extent to which wages may be garnisheed, and it further prohibits the discharge of employees because of one instance of garnishment.

Obviously the vast majority of arbitration cases on garnishment disputes occurred before July 1970. Therefore, the case that follows has been chosen because it did not produce disciplinary action until after the second offense.

In March 1970, Kaiser Aluminum & Chemical Corporation discharged an employee whose earnings had been garnisheed. It took this action under a plant rule that prescribed verbal and written counseling for the first garnishment, a written warning for the second, a three-day suspension for the third, a written warning and a five-day suspension for the fourth, and finally discharge for a fifth garnishment for a separate debt within 18 months. The action was sustained by Arbitrator Leonard Oppenheim on the grounds that the grievant had full notice and warning of the consequences of garnishments, he had not filed bankruptcy proceedings until after the second day of his suspension for his fourth garnishment, this new company policy was substantially more liberal than that provided for in Title III, and the rule was reasonable and had been communicated generally to all employees.

This case had many of the ingredients common to those in which the employer's actions are upheld: repeated garnishments, separate debts, a reasonable and well-communicated rule, previous warnings and suspensions, and no material effort on the part of the worker to straighten out his financial affairs, even by a timely declaration of bankruptcy. It could operate in the employee's behalf in arbitration, on the other hand, if he possessed a long and clean work record or if he had no prior knowledge of the existence of the debt.[28]

MOONLIGHTING

Moonlighting rules are promulgated by a company usually for two reasons. One, as we saw in a previous section, is to keep its employees from working for a competitor and divulging trade secrets. The other is to prevent its employees from engaging in work that has a negative influence on their performance of their main jobs. It bears repeating that what an employee does on his own time is generally his own business, but that a company can legitimately concern itself with the off-premises activities if these are detrimental to its interests.

The Tribune Publishing Company was ruled to have just cause for discharging its *Oakland Tribune* drama critic, who accepted outside work as a press agent for the operator of a summer theater. The arbiter agreed with the employer's contention that the outside employment created a conflict of interest. Further, it violated a contract provision that "Without permission in writing from the Publisher, no employee shall use the name of the Publisher or his connection with the Publisher or any featured title or other material of the Publisher to exploit in any way his outside endeavor." The critic never obtained the employer's permission to act as a press agent; she did get the job through her connection with the publisher; and she allowed her name, which was also the name of her column, to be used in promoting the summer theater.[29]

An employee at the Forest City Foundries Company asked to leave work early because he was "sleepy, tired, and sick." The foreman denied the request because he did not consider fatigue an adequate excuse. An argument ensued, during which the employee threatened to hit the foreman. Later that same day, after management discussions, a termination record was signed and shown to the employee's steward, and the employee was then sent a telegram notifying him of the discharge. He filed a grievance, and it came out in the hearings that he had been working for someone else part time. The arbitrator commented:

> In the instant case the Arbitrator has concluded that the Company was justified in discharging the Grievant. Grievant had the benefit of both vigorous and conscientious defense by his Union representatives and considerate suggestions and discussions from the Company personnel director. However, his extensive moonlighting has apparently taken its toll both physically and emotionally, rendering him overly sensitive to the supervisory efforts of his Foreman and others. It is unfortunate that in an age when most workers are actively seeking constantly shorter workweeks, this Grievant found it necessary to work at a second job for "between 6 and 39 hours per week." During the week of the discharge, the Grievant worked at his second job 34 hours. It is not the responsibility of the primary Employer to absorb intemperate conduct caused by fatigue or illness brought on by moonlighting activities.[30]

Presumably the company would not have challenged the secondary work if it had not had a negative effect on the grievant's performance, attendance, and attitude. The secondary employer was not a competitor.

There are circumstances under which a person has been held to be entitled to take a job with a secondary employer when he was physically unable to work for a primary employer. For example, an employee injured his arm while working at a cemetery and could no longer do the only type of work available for him there. During the period of his idleness, he was able to take a job as a bartender because the pains in his arm, for which he later underwent an operation, did not interfere with these lighter duties. When the cemetery management discovered him working at his second job, it discharged him, only to have Arbitrator Robert L. Stutz subsequently reinstate him.[31]

A firm that supplied janitorial services to offices discharged an employee for performing similar tasks in a tavern after completing his work for the primary employer. The arbiter ruled that the discharge was not for just or proper cause. First of all, the company had no rule or established past practice prohibiting dual employment. Second, the tavern keeper was not a competitor; nor did the employee's duties involve any trade secrets or even semiskilled work. Third, though the company had complained of the quality of his work, these complaints were not related in any way to the fact that he had the other job. The arbitrator reinstated him with full seniority and back pay.[32]

Another company was held not justified in discharging an employee who refused to give up his part-time job with its competitor. The arbiter pointed out that the employee had no access to his employer's trade secrets, and there was no evidence that he had disclosed any to the competitor; the company had established no plant rule forbidding personnel to work for direct or indirect competitors even though it knew that other workers had part-time jobs similar to the grievant's; and neither the quality nor the quantity of the employee's work had suffered as a result of his moonlighting.[33]

REFUSAL TO CROSS PICKET LINES

There is little question that a company may discipline or discharge employees who engage in illegal work stoppages and strikes. In this connection, if its labor agreement contains a no-strike clause, it may impose punishment on workers who refuse to cross a picket line at another employer's place of business, which is an unprotected activity under the Labor Management Relations Act.[34]

Arbitration cases revolving on this issue reveal varying treatment.

An employer suspended workers for two days who refused to cross a picket line to perform installations at a customer's premises. Arbitrator Wayne Quinlan held that this action was not justified under the contract. The employees' refusal was not a "strike, concerted plan for absence from work, or lockout," which the agreement banned, but was rather "lawful activity," with which the company had agreed not to interfere in its recognition clause. Moreover, the suspensions were not justified as a preservation of "efficient operation of its business," for no particular urgency attached to this job and the company had assigned no other workers to it but waited until the suspended employees had returned to work.[35]

Where the established picket line is that of another union, the right of employees to refuse to cross it may be determined by the language of their own agreement.

For example, in a dispute involving Sears, Roebuck and Co., the company was held by Arbiter Arthur Miller to have violated the contract's no-lockout provisions when it would not reinstate employees who respected another union's picket lines. The contract in effect permitted workers to do this and provided for them to be placed on leaves of absence and to exercise their contractual seniority rights to regain jobs filled by replacements. Their action thus did not constitute ground for discharge.[36]

Joseph T. Ryerson & Son, Inc. disciplined employees for participating in an "illegal strike" when they refused to cross another union's picket lines. Arbiter Edward A. Lynch ruled that the company did not have just cause. The disciplined employees had no control over the situation and did not instigate or participate in the picket line, and the company did not bring in uniformed policemen or provide other guarantees of their personal safety. Therefore, they had not violated the contract or mounted an illegal strike by refusing to cross the picket line.[37]

Arbitrator Henry W. Hoel saw the facts differently in a case involving the Hess Oil & Chemical Corp. and upheld the company's discharge of a worker who refused to cross a peaceful picket line set up at its plant by a union of which he was not a member. There was no solicitation of the company's employees by the pickets; the line was merely intended to inform the public that the employer was paying substandard wages to temporary workers; the grievant's union advised all members they could ignore the picket line because of their own contract with the company; all other employees crossed the picket line; and the worker had already been warned, because of an earlier incident in which he had stated he would never cross a threatened picket line that didn't materialize, that he would be discharged unless he reported for work.[38]

STRIKES

Employees who engage in an economic strike can be replaced by the company with impunity. In contrast, those who engage in an unfair labor practice strike must be reinstated. In fact, jobs must be made for them if need be, even if hired replacements have to be dismissed.

The *Labor Relations Expediter* of the Bureau of National Affairs provides an excellent description of strikes. It calls them organized labor's major weapon in fighting for its aim when private negotiation, conciliation, mediation, arbitration, and the orders of government agencies have failed to produce a resolution of employer-union differences. The national labor policy of this country as set forth in the LMRA is based on the right of employees to strike in concert if collective negotiations fail to provide them with what they deem satisfactory wages, hours, and working conditions.

In response to the strike weapon in an economic dispute, the employer may attempt to keep his operations going by hiring replacements for strikers. He also may put the terms that were spurned by the union into effect after a genuine impasse has been reached. Or he may anticipate a strike threat by laying off his workers.[39]

As has been observed several times, there is little question regarding a company's right to discipline and discharge workers for violating a no-strike pledge in the labor agreement. Customarily the issue before the arbitrator in disputes over company action against strikers is whether the employer was arbitrary or discriminatory in his selection of those to be disciplined or discharged. Arbiters have usually ruled that a company cannot single out an individual striker for discipline or for heavier punishment unless it can prove that he demonstrated leadership of the strike.[40]

When union officials have participated in such unlawful activity, a harsher penalty will generally be upheld on the premise that this is a graver offense for them than for the ordinary employee.[41] Not only must union officials refrain from engaging in "negative leadership"; some arbiters hold that they have an obligation, by virtue of their union position, to demonstrate "affirmative leadership" in opposition to any contractual violations by employees.[42]

Whether participation in a wildcat strike justifies the company's denying strikers all the protective provisions of the contract is an unsettled question among arbitrators. Some practitioners have ruled that workers have terminated their service under the contract by participating in an illegal strike.[43] One concluded that violation of the no-strike article did not terminate the contract and that participants did not cease to be employees.[44] Another arbiter held that an employer was free to ignore the seniority and recall provisions of the contract when resuming operations after a strike when no claim was made that the recall process adopted was discriminatory.[45]

Misconduct During Strikes

Arbitrators are nearly unanimous in holding that employees who engage in misconduct during a strike, whether a legal or an illegal work stoppage, are properly subject to discipline or discharge. The offenses often occur in connection with management's exercise of its legal right to continue to operate its enterprise during a strike. More often than not, they consist of violence, threats, and intimidation perpetrated against workers who continue to enter the employer's premises during the strike and perform their jobs, which is also a legal right.

Arbitrator J. Fred Holly discussed the labor practitioner's responsibility in cases like this to determine what penalty should be considered appropriate to the crime:

> A strike situation embraces an environment vastly different [from] that which exists in the daily relations of the parties. Generally, the workaday principle that discharge is for just cause if it is not arbitrary, capricious or discriminatory has obvious shortcomings when applied to employees' action during strikes. In the latter situation there is an absence of supervision; the atmosphere is emotionally charged, particularly if the Employer exercises his right to keep the plant open; there is a more ready availability of remedies at law; community attitudes and pressures bring an added force to bear on the parties; and all of these factors are increased in intensity in a first strike situation such as the subject one. As a consequence, acts of indiscretion and violence are to be more expected during strikes. Yet, the expectation of incidents of violence does not remove the need for or the right to discipline. Violence is not to be condoned except under the most unusual circumstances. Given the aforementioned differences, however, disciplinary action short of discharge may be required in a strike situation, even though a similar act might warrant discharge in a normal work situation. Therefore, it is incumbent upon the Arbitrator to examine all circumstances that exist in the strike situation before deciding upon the propriety of the discipline administered.[46]

The Westinghouse Electric Corporation satisfied the arbiter of a dispute arising out of a wildcat strike that its discipline, which was "short of discharge," was appropriate. The strike began when employees failed to return to work after the lunch break. Pickets appeared at the plant gates about 2:00 P.M., and on the following morning all entrances to the plant were barricaded. An employee who normally reported to work about 2:45 P.M. came in early, at 1:30, to recover some insurance due him. He had no knowledge that pickets were at the gates since he was inside the plant at the time the picket lines formed. He reported to his regular job, noting only that several of his fellow employees were absent. When he left the plant in his car at 11:45 that evening, a black sedan started to follow him. The sedan tried to pull alongside, first on one side and then on the other. When it finally succeeded in doing so, its occupants threw several rocks or heavy objects at the right side of his car, at least two of them striking and breaking the glass in two windows. There was sufficient light from street lamps for the worker to identify the people in the sedan.

After he reported the incident to a supervisor, one of the offending employees was given a 10-day disciplinary suspension and two others were each given a 5-day suspension. Arbitrator Al T. Singletary upheld the company's action.[47]

At the General American Transportation Corporation, management imposed three-day disciplinary suspensions on 18 of 45 employees who engaged in a strike in violation of the contract. Arbitrator Harry Abrahams ruled that the discipline was not discriminatory since the 18 employees either picketed the plant or were union officers who acted as spokesmen for the strikers. The 27 workers who were exempted were not on the picket line and did not actively participate in keeping the employees out on strike. The arbitrator considered that the company in this matter was very lenient as it had authority under the contract to impose the discharge penalty but instead chose to exact only a three-day suspension.[48]

The misconduct of employees during an economic strike at a hospital took the form of sitdowns in the hospital administrator's office. This activity willfully violated a state court order prohibiting strikers from trespassing on hospital premises. Moreover, it was designed to force the hospital to recognize a union that had been unable to establish its majority status before the state court. The company discharged the participants.

The doctrine of the NLRB in a case involving Fansteel Inc. was of interest to the arbiter in this connection. At Fansteel, a group of employees seized and held two key buildings. The Supreme Court of the United States supported the discharge of the employees, stating: "We are unable to conclude that Congress intended to compel employers to retain persons in their employ regardless of their unlawful conduct" or "to invest those who go on strike with an immunity from discharge for acts of trespass. . . ."[49] A comment of the arbitrator in the hospital dispute is instructive: "Violence is implicit in the very act of sitting down; no matter that there is no additional violence committed in its execution." The arbiter held that those engaged in the sitdown were guilty of serious misconduct and should be disciplined.[50]

The opinion of an arbitrator in a General Electric Company case is perhaps unique and certainly representative of a minority viewpoint. In this dispute, the company imposed disciplinary suspensions on three union members for picket-line misconduct during an economic strike. The arbiter held that the employer's actions were not for just cause because in his opinion the company's right to exercise its disciplinary function was operative *only* during the time the employee was obligated to contribute to production. Since an economic strike was in progress, the workers were therefore freed of this obligation. It was also significant to him that the company had kept its plant gates open and operated its business during the work stoppage. In this connection he commented:

> Under the circumstances the Company's right to discipline employees engaged in an illegal strike where it itself is a contributor to a violence-provoking environment can only be judged against the same criteria that are invoked by any citizen who takes measures to defend his property in a civil disturbance. The criteria of judgment expected are much more vigorous than in ordinary cases of alleged employee misbehavior under normal conditions.[51]

The arbiter concluded that the three disciplined employees should be reinstated with full back pay.

Holdings such as this are rare, and this seems fortunate. It is regrettable that when a company exercises its legal right to operate its business or an employee his right to pursue his livelihood, some perceive such a justifiable act as irresponsible and unreasonably provocative of the illegal conduct of others.

UNION ACTIVITIES

Generally speaking, the most delicate type of discharge or discipline case is the one that centers on a union officer as the target of management's action. His dual role, as an employee and as an official of the labor organization, adds a dimension to his conduct that the acts of other employees do not have. As an employee, he has only the rights and privileges of other rank-and-file workers within his bargaining unit and is governed by the same rules and regulations they must heed. But as a union representative, he enjoys a certain latitude in his day-to-day application and implementation of the contract. Moreover, he becomes coequal with the company's supervisors, which enables him to represent the positions and interests of his constituents effectively and vigorously.[52]

Management's discipline or discharge of a union official frequently raises the question of whether he performed his act in the capacity of an employee or a union representative and, if the latter, what special consideration or immunity he should be entitled to. Often, too, management's action is challenged with the allegation that it had an antiunion or discriminatory motivation. Such was the situation in a dispute decided by Arbitrator Whitley P. McCoy, who articulated these concepts in his finding:

There is a clear distinction between the case of a supervisor telling an employee to go back on his job and a supervisor telling the Union to stop investigating a grievance. The Company and Union have met on equal terms and adopted a Contract recognizing each other's rights. Each has its dignity to uphold. Organizations and corporations can act only through agents and representatives. When the duly authorized representative of the Company told the duly authorized representative of the Union to stop investigating a grievance, it was the Company issuing an order to the Union. . . . If [the Steward] could rightly be penalized, it would put the entire grievance machinery, set up by the Agreement of the parties at the highest levels, at the mercy of Supervisors with the possibility of great harm to the relations of the parties, even to a complete breakdown of the grievance machinery.[53]

The Union Official's Greater Responsibility

It is generally recognized by arbitrators that local union officials not only have the same responsibility as other employees to perform their regular jobs satisfactorily but also carry the additional burden of enforcing the contract and influencing other workers to comply with its terms. For example, as the section on strikes discussed briefly, a union official who engages in an unauthorized work stoppage is committing a graver offense than are rank-and-file participants.[54] By virtue of his office, he is a leader; indeed, it is reasonable to assume that he has acquired his union position because he is a leader. It follows inescapably that when he participates in a work stoppage, even makes no effort to prevent it or bring it to a close, he is setting an example for the other employees and indicating expressly or tacitly that the stoppage has his approval. Because his influence is broader than his fellow workers', so is his responsibility.

This concept was voiced by Arbitrator Arthur Miller in a decision settling a dispute over the suspension of a shop steward for engaging in a strike in violation of his company's labor agreement:

The proposition that affirmative obligations of leadership in upholding the grievance procedure and opposing work stoppages devolve upon an employee who . . . as a Union officer must be held to have achieved a position of influence has hitherto found acceptance under this and other agreements. Implicit in it is the thought that if those prominent and influential in the affairs of the Union fail to so support these vital provisions of the Agreement, the parties' expectations that they will be complied with during the life of the Agreement become altogether illusory.[55]

Some arbitrators have even viewed a union official's passivity in the face of known violations of the contract by employees as a type of "negative leadership." One such opinion was expressed by Arbitrator Pearce Davis in a case involving penalties imposed on the local union president, committeeman, and shop steward for not attempting to prevent an unauthorized work stoppage. Arbiter Davis said:

> Local Union officials are the spokesmen for the workers. They are their leaders. They, therefore, have responsibilities over and beyond those of the rank and file. Local Union officials are obligated aggressively to oppose actions that violate commitments undertaken in good faith. Local Union officials are bound by virtue of their office to set personal examples of opposition to contract violations. They cannot be passive; they must vigorously seek to prevent contract violations by their constituents.[56]

Countermanding Management's Orders

The authority of union representatives, broad though it is, stops short at the threshold of management's functions. There appears to be near unanimity among arbitrators that it is improper for union officials to countermand management's orders as long as these deal with matters generally falling within its domain. Harry Shulman articulated this wisdom in one of his many cases when he said:

> No committeeman or other Union officer is entitled to instruct employees to disobey Supervision's orders no matter how strongly he may believe that the orders are in violation of the Agreement. If he believes that an improper order has been issued, his course is to take the matter up with the Supervision and to seek to effect an adjustment. Failing to effect an adjustment, he may file a grievance. But he may not tell the employee to disregard the order.[57]

In a similar dispute, although Arbitrator Feinberg reduced a discharge to suspension, he strongly censured a union shop chairman and said:

> Certainly, a shop chairman has no right to countermand instructions given by Management's representatives, whether or not he believes those instructions contrary to the terms of the collective bargaining agreement. . . . Any other arrangement would result in a chaotic condition in the plant and seriously interfere with production.[58]

The overwhelming majority of arbitral opinions reflect the view that an industrial plant is not a debating society. When controversies arise, as they inevitably will, the operation of the enterprise must go on while the dispute is being discussed and resolved. The authority to direct the operation vests solely in management. The grievance procedure is designed to rectify abuses of supervisory authority, and the remedy under the labor agreement for violation of rights lies in the grievance and arbitration provisions only. No union representative or individual employee may disregard or countermand a supervisor's orders. The only exception to this is a directive to perform an act that is unlawful or immoral or that would jeopardize the health, safety, or welfare of other employees.

These contingencies aside, the union representative's posture should be that the employee is obliged to obey the supervisor's instructions and seek redress if need be through the grievance procedure. The efficient and orderly operation of a plant requires that employees and union officers alike respect management's authority. And union representatives who advise workers to circumvent or disobey instructions open themselves to possible disciplinary action.

Insubordination by Union Officials

In cases involving alleged insubordination by union officeholders, penalties are considered properly the same as for rank-and-file employees under similar circumstances if the official was insubordinate *as an employee.*

This viewpoint was reflected in a decision on a case involving the Dominion Electric Corp., which fired a union official for refusing a job assignment related to his tasks as an employee. Arbitrator Jerome Gross concluded that the company did not discharge him with intent to discriminate.[59]

In a case involving a steward who was disciplined for leaving his work station without permission, the arbitrator overturned the suspension because plant practice permitted stewards to go to the foreman for purposes of grievance investigation and handling without first obtaining permission. It was the opinion of this arbitrator that it is

. . . unrealistic to strictly interpret the Contract to the effect that the Committeeman, learning of a grievance arising within his department and jurisdiction as a Union representative, must remain at his machine until the Foreman comes to his machine and the Committeeman is able to request permission to leave his machine to work on the grievance.[60]

Arbitrator Dudley Whiting applied a new and different type of remedy to a dispute over a union committeeman's discharge for refusing to perform assigned work that he believed was not covered by his classification. The arbiter, concluding that the committeeman's trouble was due to overzealousness in his union functions, reinstated him without back pay on the condition that he resign from his union office and pledge to remain out of that position.[61]

American Can Company, on the other hand, was found to have been justified in having discharged a union president for "gross and defiant insubordination" after he had repeatedly left his bargaining unit job without proper supervisory permission to investigate grievances.[62]

At Chrysler Corporation, under a contract that obligated the chief steward to tell his foreman the number and nature of grievances he wished to investigate, management was also found to have properly discharged the man after he had refused to perform unit overtime work because he was investigating grievances but had declined to identify them. It was significant that he had been warned he would be fired unless he either revealed the specific grievances under investigation or returned to the job.[63]

In another case, the arbitrator upheld the discharge of a union steward who continually carried on union activities outside of a contractually fixed time period for stewards to handle grievances and other duties of office.[64]

Arbitrator Israel Ben Scheiber also supported the discharge of a union steward in a similar case. The steward had received many warnings for violating a contract ban on unauthorized union activities during working hours. He was fired when he again took working time on union matters that should have been handled by the union's financial secretary in accordance with an established and satisfactory procedure. In discussing the employee's misconduct, Arbitrator Scheiber remarked:

> We have here the case of an overzealous Department Steward with little or no understanding of the intelligent use of authority imposed on him by his fellow workers.
>
> In the opinion of the Arbitrator, he was guilty of a serious disservice to his fellow workers in that he needlessly gave rise to irritation and friction which especially, if repeated, must inevitably result in injury to the morale and productive efficiency of the plant as well as to good Labor-Management relations.
>
> It cannot be pointed out too often that the position of a Steward is an important one, and that the individual filling the office should be a person who, while carrying out the important responsibilities of his office and protecting the rights of his fellow workers, is nevertheless able to retain

the respect and good will of Management by the exercise not merely of zeal alone but also of good common sense.[65]

Other Rules Violations

Naturally insubordination is not the only offense for which union representatives may find themselves subjected to discipline. In their employee functions, as noted a number of times, all plant rules and other regulatory conditions that govern the behavior of workers apply to them also and in equal measure. Union officials have found themselves in serious trouble with management for their transgressions in a number of areas.

Absenteeism. Where lies the proper balance between the work-time latitude provided a union official and his obligations as an employee? This was the question facing Arbitrator Harry Seligson in a hearing between Cessna Aircraft Co. and the International Association of Machinists over the discharge of a union president for absenteeism. In examining the situation, the arbiter made the following determination:

> The Grievant was out an inordinate number of days for a variety of reasons: outside Union business, illness, personal reasons. He was warned repeatedly about this, even to the extent of being given a disciplinary layoff. Although he was not occupying a key job in the department, it was a job necessary to the general operation of the department. Knowing that the Company took a serious view of his absences and his leaving the job without first securing permission, he made little effort after the disciplinary layoff to comply with the reasonable requirements expected of him, but continued to absent himself on Union business, aware on the basis of his previous record that the chances were good he might also be out for illness. Under these circumstances I consider that the Company has justified its charge of excessive absenteeism. The grievance is denied.[66]

Altercations and abuse. Despite the relaxed and loose usage of shop vernacular, arbitrators have upheld discharges of union officials for insulting, abusive, and intimidating attacks on members of management.[67] An employee who dislikes his supervisors has limitations on how far he can go in demonstrating it. When that employee is also a union representative, his conduct and behavior should be somewhat more restrained.

This was the view of Arbitrator Eli Rock in upholding the discharge of a steward who abused his authority. After being demoted, this employee filed a number of grievances, several contending that the demotion was punitive and another alleging that his supervisor cursed the men, was discriminatory, and was unfit to be a boss. Arbitrator Rock decided that here was more than merely an overzealous steward; here was a man whose behavior patterns exceeded the reasonable boundaries of a union representative's conduct in a plant. In rendering this award, he stated that mere zeal or militancy would not have justified discipline. But the steward's repeated and unfounded written accusations of a criminal or semicriminal nature against management personnel, his threats of physical violence in retaliation, and his public bullying tactics could not be condoned by a finding in his favor. Upholding this grievance would indicate some degree of approval of conduct that would place the plant's collective bargaining relationship on a jungle level.[68]

In a somewhat similar situation at Chrysler Corporation, the company was found to be justified in discharging a union chief steward for filing a grievance in which he charged a supervisor with manhandling another employee, since the evidence indicated that the grievance was baseless.[69] On the other hand, an employer was not sustained in his attempt to discharge a union official who personally instigated the filing of a large number of grievances.[70]

Drinking. Arbitrator Charles G. Hampton encountered the problem of the discharge of two union officials who drank on the job and on company premises one Christmas Eve. In this decision, he observed that drinking on the job was dangerous to the two employees themselves and their fellow workers and that it was also a direct violation of the contract. The union argued that the company had failed to detect other employees guilty of the same offense, but the arbiter ruled that this consideration was immaterial. He sustained the discharge action.[71]

Falsification. Arbitrator David A. Wolff was faced with the problem of the discharge of a newly elected union officer for falsification of his employment application. Although the officer was militant and aggressive, and his discharge followed by one day the union's strike vote on grievances he had been processing, Wolff found that the company's action was not discriminatory or premised on his union activities. In his decision, he commented: "Whether or not he had been a Union official his falsification would have supported discharge. That he was a Union official would not [militate] against the impropriety of what he had done. . . . The grievance is dismissed." [72]

Arbitrator Harold M. Gilden found the discharge of a union steward to be a warranted exercise of a managerial discretion when the company established to his satisfaction that the steward was guilty of submitting false piecework tickets, thus claiming additional compensation for work that he was unable to prove he had performed in his bargaining unit assignment.[73]

Gambling. Gambling on company time and on company premises is another violation for which a union representative can be disciplined. In deciding the case described in Chapter 4 of the local union officer who was discharged for operating baseball and numbers pools at work, the arbitrator stated:

> Patently the issue here is whether the Grievant was discharged for just cause or if, as the Union charges, the dismissal was capricious and discriminatory. The Company avers the discipline meted out was just and proper because:
>
> (1) all four types of gambling games conducted by the Grievant violated the criminal code and had they adopted a laissez-faire policy and closed their eyes to such violations they could have been ejected from their premises by the very terms of the lease agreement;
>
> (2) Rule 6 of the Company Rules and Regulations provides immediate dismissal for gambling;
>
> (3) the gambling activities conducted by the Grievant had adversely affected plant productivity as is evidenced by substantial productive improvement after the Grievant's discharge and gambling ceased.
>
> The Arbitrator, on the basis of the testimony adduced, is constrained to find that the Grievant did conduct gambling activities on the Company premises in violation of Rule 6 and his discharge was for just cause.[74]

Jokes. A union president was discharged by Art Metal Works Inc. for preparing a company order to remove exterior plant floodlights, signing it with the plant superintendent's name, and filing the form as a legitimate order. It proved unavailing for him to allege that his intent was merely to play a joke on a night watchman; in Arbitrator Benjamin S. Kirsh's view, the faked order might have resulted in a loss of company property by fire or theft, and this made the offense a serious one. In commenting on the effect of a union president's discharge on the relationship between the parties, the arbitrator stated:

> It was contended on the part of the Union that L_____ had been a long-time faithful and competent employee of the Company and that he had been a Union member from the time that the Union had first been recognized by the Company, and was, in effect, President of the Union at the time of his discharge. . . .
>
> An argument directed to the responsibility of a member of the Union carries with it a correlative argument that such responsibility also implies

an obligation on the part of an important member of the Union to be an example to fellow Union members in orderly and considerate dealing with Management. Inhering in an act of subscribing a plant superintendent's name to an order is a lack of respect by the leader of the Union for the normal management-union relationship. . . . The example set for the general workers in the plant is not conducive to a sound management-labor relationship and mutual respect in their varied dealings.[75]

Ignorance of the Law Is an Excuse

It is not uncommon for arbitrators to weigh the length of time an offender has held union office and consider his degree of sophistication and familiarity with the scope of his union authority. They often hold that a new steward's improprieties may be wholly or partly excused by the fact that he is not completely informed.

Such was the finding in an International Harvester case concerning a union committeeman who was disciplined for violating a rule forbidding the distribution of handbills on company property. He had acted in the honest belief that he was within his rights because a recent NLRB decision had found another company's order prohibiting the distribution of union leaflets on company parking lots illegal.[76]

Arbitrator Clarence Updegraff went a step further in resolving a dispute over a discharged steward who, on his first day in office, had told his foreman he was entitled to go where he pleased and proceeded to roam up and down in disregard of the foreman's repeated orders. Although Updegraff censured the steward's overall behavior, he considered that the man

> . . . would nevertheless have taken immediate proper directions from his own chief within the Union, the Divisional Steward. However, this opportunity to give the inexperienced Steward timely correction was ignored by the Foreman. The green Steward was given a further opportunity to repeat his mistake and to sink further into the consequences of his blunder. . . . Modern personnel relations require from both sides and their representatives at least a reasonable degree of sympathetic tolerance. On the night of the dispute, S_____ was an inexperienced, newly appointed Steward. Management appears to have been guilty almost of entrapment of the Steward into a harsh consequence of an ignorant mistake, instead of cooperating in a charitable and tolerant effort to correct his erroneous assumptions.[77]

Although most labor practitioners don't go quite so far as Arbitrator Updegraff, the majority usually give ample consideration to the factor of inexperience. Raymond Hayes joined this majority by reinstating discharged union officers even though the evidence established that they had instigated and participated in a strike in violation of the contract. He reached his decision in view of the mitigating circumstances that the union officers were inexperienced; the employer's operations, local union, and contract were new; and accumulated grievances had caused employee unrest.[78]

By virtue of his office, a representative of the union has a special obligation to observe and respect its agreement with his company. It is his contractually recognized function to protect employees through the grievance procedure against violations of that agreement by management. The agreement gives him special rights and privileges so that he may perform his role. He cannot turn his back with impunity on the very contract that it is his duty to defend.

Chapter 6
Union-Imposed Discipline

Many labor agreements contain a union security provision requiring employees to become members of the union and maintain their membership in good standing as a condition of continued employment. Such agreements often include as well a clause providing for the company to deduct dues from workers' earnings. The labor organization is entitled to call for the discharge of an employee who fails to join the union and authorize these payments.

A typical example of a union security clause providing for both a union shop and dues deductions is the following:

1.01.   It shall be a condition of employment that all employees on the payroll as of the effective date of this Agreement shall become members of the Union on or after the 31st day following the execution of this Agreement and shall maintain their membership in the Union for the duration of the Agreement to the extent of paying an initiation fee and the periodic dues uniformly required as a condition of retaining membership in the local Union.

1.02.   Furthermore, [the same requirements shall apply to] all employees hired on or after the effective date of this Agreement . . . [beginning] the 31st day following their employment. . . .

1.03.   The provision for the payment of an initiation fee and membership dues will be satisfied by the offer or tender of the initiation fee and membership dues uniformly required of all Union members.

1.04.   The Company agrees that it will, during the term of this Agreement, deduct monthly Union dues and initiation fees from the earnings of those employees certified as members of the Union when notice of membership is accompanied by an individually signed card authorizing the Company to deduct such Union dues. The Company further agrees that it will deduct delinquent monthly Union dues from the earnings of each employee upon the employee's signing an appropriate form, which the Company shall provide and submit to the employee. It is specifically understood that this practice must at all times conform to applicable and authorized state and federal laws.

1.05. Any check-off dues authorization will be canceled automatically if the employee ceases to be employed in the bargaining unit, or the Union is no longer the duly certified bargaining representative of the employees, or if an applicable collective bargaining agreement expires and has not been renewed or extended, or a succeeding collective bargaining agreement has not been executed prior to said expiration.

Most contracts also contain a clause relating to probationary employees. It customarily stipulates a period during which the new worker is solely under the employer's jurisdiction and is not covered by any of the provisions of the labor agreement. More often than not, the probation period is identical to the time within which the new employee must obtain union membership.

STATUTORY REGULATIONS

The United States Supreme Court has noted that the Labor Management Relations Act, section 8(a)(3), has given the labor organization the right to bargain a union shop agreement with the employer under which it may seek to have employees fired for failing to pay initiation fees or dues. But "the power to cause the discharge of employees for any other reason" is withheld by the LMRA.[1] Moreover, it has been held by lower courts that a union was forbidden to ask for the dismissal of workers who were delinquent in their dues when there was no union security clause in effect.[2] Also, fines have been distinguished legally from initiation fees and dues: the U.S. Court of Appeals at San Francisco upheld an NLRB ruling that a union could not lawfully require the discharge of a member who failed to pay a fine even though it did have a union security agreement with the company. This was the ruling despite the fact that the fine might have been called for under union rules that the employee might have violated.[3]

Companies that fall under the provisions of the Taft Act must be careful in acceding to a union request to fire a worker whom the union has expelled from membership even if this occurs under a collective bargaining agreement containing a union shop clause. The expulsion is not sufficient ground for discharge unless it has in turn been caused by his refusal to pay dues or initiation fees.

In this connection, the National Labor Relations Board is empowered to decide whether initiation fees are too high. The facts of each case determine what the Board may consider to be excessive. However, the Taft Act provides some guidance in stating that consideration should be given to, among other things, the practices and customs of labor unions in the particular industry and the wages being paid to the affected employees.

In addition to setting its fees and dues, a union enjoys the right under the Taft Act to make its own rules on other internal matters. The Board has ruled that the union may invoke such rules except where the action would interfere with a member's employment rights under the law. A provision of the act also allows the union to require a member to exhaust internal remedies before instituting a grievance action against it. But the Board has held that this rule might not be enforced through fines against members for filing unfair labor practice charges.[4]

The Landrum-Griffin Act comes into play when a union is attempting to discipline a member for reasons other than nonpayment of dues. This act requires that the labor organization follow certain procedures and allows the worker to seek relief in federal courts if they are not followed, though union members still have the liberty to contest the discipline in state courts. A number of courts have ruled that "appropriate relief" includes the recovery of damages directly and proximately resulting from union violations of the Landrum-Griffin Act.[5]

THE SCOPE OF UNION AUTHORITY

The discipline a union imposes on members may assume a variety of forms. It may consist of fines; it may involve a threat not to handle members' grievances; or it may be suspension or expulsion if the misconduct is extremely serious in the eyes of the union.

Management usually has no right to intervene either to support or to oppose disciplinary action for violation of any union rules and bylaws except those concerning the payment of fees and dues, as discussed.

Despite this limitation, unions have attempted to cause discharges for a variety of other offenses. Regardless of whether a valid union security agreement existed, the courts have barred such union efforts in the following representative cases:

1. Where a member engaged in activity in the plant which the union claimed was antiunion in character.[6]
2. Where a member failed to attend union meetings called by the local's officers.[7]
3. Where a member mounted political opposition to the local's business agent and secretary-treasurer.[8]
4. Where an employee negotiated more favorable conditions for himself with the company than were provided in its labor agreement with the union.[9]
5. Conversely, where a member accepted a wage rate lower than the union's scale.[10]

As management may not intrude on the union's rights, so the labor organization may not encroach on the employer's preserves. But there is a troublesome gray area encompassing the job activities of a union member who is in a supervisory position, and these may provoke company-union disputes that are brought to arbitration. The majority of the rare arbitration hearings on union discipline of members involve publishing firms and newspapers in contests with typographical unions. This may be explained in part by the fact that labor agreements between these parties commonly call for foremen to be union members as well. These employees often find themselves walking a thin line between their obligations as supervisors and semimembers of management and their loyalty to the labor organization. When the union's expectations of allegiance from them are not fulfilled, it will be likely to attempt to impose some disciplinary penalty.

The question of loyalty to the union actually underlies all the specific issues to be discussed next, but they are divided into the aspects of the member's work life that the labor organization is authorized to oversee.

Dues and Fees

A union expelled a member for activities furthering the interests of a rival union. When it later affiliated with the rival, the worker was advised that his expulsion still stood. Then he was told that he would be permitted to join the new organization provided he paid an initiation fee of $100. He first refused but later joined under protest when the union attempted to obtain his discharge following its successful negotiation of a union shop clause. The matter went before the NLRB, which ruled that the fee requirement was lawful.[11]

In another case, however, the Board brought a contrary finding. An employee stopped paying dues when he went to work for a nonunion firm, which prompted the labor organization to suspend him. Later, when he took a job with another company that had a union security agreement, the union informed him that he owed $674 in back dues but said that it would accept $286, an amount equal to its initiation fee, for reinstatement. When he refused to pay either amount, the union invoked its security clause to cause his discharge. Its argument was that it was only imposing a valid reinstatement fee. The NLRB disagreed, calling the action a "camouflaged attempt" to collect back dues that had accrued at a time when the worker was not obligated to maintain membership.[12]

Employment Duties

The International Mailers Union filed charges of conduct unbecoming a member against a mail room foreman for his role in installing a new bulk delivery system. The employer, the Memphis Publishing Company, had a labor agreement with the union providing that "The foreman shall be responsible to the employer only." The issue went before Arbitrator Clair V. Duff, who ruled that the foreman had merely implemented the change as directed by management. Although it was the union's view that the new delivery system was detrimental to bargaining unit personnel, Arbiter Duff reasoned that the exercise of valid managerial authority could not be limited by the union's threatening or carrying out the discipline of a foreman who was a union member. Accordingly, he ruled that the charges against the foreman should be dropped.[13]

The collective bargaining agreement between the Journal Company and the Milwaukee Typographical Union provided that the composing room foreman and assistant foreman be union members. It also stipulated that [the] Union shall not discipline the Foreman or Assistant Foreman for carrying out the instructions of the Publisher or his representatives as authorized by this Contract, provided that the Union shall have the right to appeal the actions of the Foreman or Assistant Foreman to the Publisher . . . or . . . [a] joint standing committee.[14]

The union brought charges of conduct unbecoming a member against a foreman and assistant foreman who had threatened to withdraw noncontract privileges from fellow union members. Arbitrator Russell A. Smith ruled that the union could not discipline the two men under the contractual language just quoted for any action they undertook while engaged in supervisory work in the composing room unless the publisher had expressly prohibited the action and had made the prohibition known to the union.[15]

In a dispute between the Publishers Association of New York City and the New York Typographical Union, the union had called a strike after the contract had expired. The composing room foreman, a union member, had taken steps to close down the composing room in an orderly way after the strike was called. Because the agreement had expired, the arbitrator ruled that the union could discipline the foreman even though he may have acted in the sincere belief that his conduct was necessary to protect the employer and had not intended to injure the cause of the union.[16]

One of the few arbitration cases involving an employer and union not in the publishing industry arose out of a dispute between the New York Twist Drill Corp. and the Teamsters. Their labor agreement contained a provision stating that "Either party to this agreement shall be permitted to call employee witnesses at each and every step of the grievance and arbitration procedure." In accordance with this clause, the company used four union members to testify as its witnesses at an arbitration hearing on a discharge. The union reacted by fining them $75 each and suspending their right to hold union office for two years. Arbitrator Edgar J. Nathan concluded that the discipline was a direct result of their testifying and found no support for the union's contention that their evidence had been given in bad faith. He therefore ruled that the union was prohibited from enforcing any disciplinary measures against the four men, and he directed it to revoke the fines.[17]

Picketing

The NLRB has reasoned that a union's general right to enforce internal rules allows it specifically to fine members who refuse to perform picket line duty. An illustrative case concerns a union member who was fined $500 for his refusal to picket and brought charges with the Board that he had been restrained and coerced in the exercise of his right to refrain from picketing. The NLRB conceded that the fine did constitute a form of coercion but not of the type prohibited under the Taft Act. Since the union had a rule that governed the trial and fining of members found guilty of "gross disobedience," the NLRB held that imposing such fines did not violate the law.[18]

Courts have upheld union fines levied on members for crossing picket lines and going to work. Similarly, the Board has ruled that a union was not in violation of the law when it demanded the payment of such fines and finally instituted state court proceedings to collect them. The Board found it significant in this case that the union made no effort to affect its members' job rights, and it commented that "When a strike is lawful and the picket line is lawful, we cannot hold that a union must take no steps to preserve its own integrity.[19]

NLRB decisions such as this one have been upheld by the U.S. Supreme Court. The view it expressed in one case was that the legal prohibition on union restraint and coercion is not intended to reach union attempts to enforce, through fines and court actions, legitimate rules against members' crossing picket lines. The law permits unions to enforce such rules by expelling a member and the Court reasoned that the imposition of fines is a less coercive discipline.[20]

Production Quotas

Unions have occasionally fined members who exceeded union-established production quotas. On this issue, the NLRB and the courts are not in accord in their decisions.

With the sanction of the U.S. Court of Appeals at Chicago, the NLRB held in one dispute that a union had operated within its rights in establishing rules for maximum levels of piecework production and then fining members who violated them by producing more than the maximum. The Board considered that the union's action was protected under the law as an internal union matter and that it did not threaten the workers' job rights.[21]

On the other hand, the U.S. Court of Appeals at San Francisco held in a case that the Taft Act clauses giving unions the right to establish their own rules do not allow them to set production ceilings. In the view of this court, rules dealing with production quotas relate to employment conditions and not to union membership. Accordingly, it concluded that the union had violated its bargaining duty to the employer by establishing production quotas without negotiating with the company. It was also significant to the court that these rules were contrary to the existing labor agreement. It appeared to the court as well that the union might have been guilty of attempting to modify the labor agreement without giving the prior notices required by law.[22]

Representation of Employees

The Dallas Typographical Union fined a member working as a foreman who refused to allow a union representative to attend a meeting between him and an employee. The labor agreement with the *Dallas Morning News,* which required foremen to join the union, protected them from union discipline for "carrying out the instructions of the Publisher as authorized by this Contract." Despite the company's assertion that it did issue "instructions" with respect to the foreman's action, Arbitrator Murray M. Rohman held that the contract did not contain and past practice negated any authorization for the exclusion of union representatives from discussions between foremen and employees.[23]

On the opposite side of the coin, the NLRB has ruled that a union threat not to handle the grievances of members who failed to pay certain assessments amounted to unlawful restraint and coercion, for the processing of members' grievances is not an internal matter and therefore is not governed by the union's right to make its own rules. As the exclusive representative of a bargaining unit, the Board concluded, the union has the obligation to accept all grievances submitted to it by the employees it bargains for and to process them impartially and without discrimination.[24]

Appendix A

Specimen Forms of Shop Rules

The following specimens of shop rules have been excerpted verbatim from various contracts. Identification has been supplied where it was available.

SPECIMEN 1

Agreement between the Delco Radio Division of General Motors Corp. and the UAW.

Shop Rules

The purpose of these rules and regulations is not to restrict the rights of anyone, but to define them and protect the rights of all and insure cooperation.

Committing any of the following violations will be sufficient grounds for disciplinary action ranging from reprimand to immediate discharge, depending upon the seriousness of the offense in the judgment of management.

1. Falsification of personnel or other records.
2. Ringing the clock card of another.
3. Repeated failure to ring own card.
4. Using another's badge or pass, or permitting another to use your badge or pass to enter the property.
5. Failure to carry badge on your person at all times while on company premises.
6. Absence without reasonable cause.
7. Reporting late for work.

8. Absence of three working days without properly notifying management.
9. Leaving own department or the plant during working hours without permission.
10. Distracting the attention of others, or causing confusion by unnecessary shouting, catcalls or demonstration in the plant.
11. Littering or contributing to poor housekeeping [or] unsanitary or unsafe conditions on plant premises.
12. Possession of weapons on Company premises at any time.
13. Refusal to obey orders of foremen or other supervision.
14. Refusal or failure to do job assignment. (Do the work assigned to you and follow instructions; any complaint may be taken up later through the regular channels.)
15. Unauthorized operation of machines, tools or equipment.
16. Making scrap unnecessarily or careless workmanship.
17. Horseplay, scuffling, running or throwing things.
18. Wasting time or loitering in toilets or on any Company property during working hours.
19. Smoking except in specifically designated areas and during specified periods.
20. Threatening, intimidating, coercing or interfering with employees or supervision at any time.
21. Unauthorized soliciting or collecting contributions for any purpose whatsoever during working time.
22. Unauthorized distribution of literature, written or printed matter of any description in working areas on Company premises during working time.
23. Posting or removal of notices, signs or writing in any form on bulletin boards or Company property at any time without specific [authorization from] management.
24. Misuse or removal from the premises without proper authorization of employee lists, blueprints, Company records or confidential information of any nature.
25. Gambling [or playing a] lottery or any other game of chance on Company premises at any time.
26. Abuse, misuse or deliberate destruction of Company property, tools [or] equipment or the property of employees in any manner.
27. Restricting output.
28. The making or publishing of false, vicious or malicious statements concerning any employee, supervisor, the Company or its products.
29. Abusive language to any employee or supervision.
30. Fighting on the premises at any time.
31. Theft or misappropriation of property of employees or of the Company.
32. Possession of or drinking of liquor or any alcoholic beverage on Company property at any time. Reporting for work under [the] influence of

alcohol, when suffering from alcoholic hangover, or in any unsafe condition.
33. Sabotage.
34. Disregard of safety rules or common safety practices.
35. Assignment of wages or frequent garnishments.
36. Immoral conduct or indecency.
37. Throwing refuse or objects on the floors or out the windows.
38. Stopping work or making preparations to leave work (such as washing up or changing clothes) before the signal sounds for lunch period or before the specified quitting time.
39. Repeated violations of shop or safety rules.
40. Failure to report all injuries, however small, to plant hospital. This applies to cuts, bruises, scratches, burns and all eye cases.

SPECIMEN 2

Agreement between Samsonite Corporation and the URW.

Whereas all of the parties to the said collective bargaining agreement have agreed that, in consideration of the Employer executing the said collective bargaining agreement, the Union and the Employer would enter into a Supplemental Agreement setting forth the grounds for discharge or other disciplinary action.

Now, therefore, it is agreed between the parties as follows:

(a) Although the Employer may impose a lesser penalty, the following shall be just cause for immediate discharge:

1. Neglect of duty.
2. Dishonesty, including falsifying of the Employer's records or making false statements when applications for employment are being made.
3. Reporting for duty under the influence of intoxicating beverages or the use or possession of intoxicating beverages on Company property at any time.
4. Destruction, abuse, removal or attempted removal of the Employer's or another employee's property or materials.
5. Engaging in a strike, picketing, sabotage or slowdown or failure or refusal to cross a picket line at the premises of the Employer or at the premises of any of the Employer's customers in connection with their work.
6. Sleeping on the job.
7. Physical violence, fighting or creating a disturbance on the Employer's premises.
8. Possession of any weapon, as defined by law, on the Employer's premises.

9. Immoral or indecent conduct on the Employer's premises.
10. Conduct which violates the common decency or morality of the community.
11. Failure to report immediately accidents or personal injury to the proper authority.
12. Falsifying or refusing to give testimony when accidents or disciplinary actions are being investigated.
13. Failure of any employee to qualify for a surety bond or revocation by the surety company of any employee's coverage under a surety bond.
14. Insubordination, including refusal or failure to perform regular, Saturday, Sunday, holiday or overtime work duly assigned.
15. Disobedience of orders or acts of disrespect toward superiors.
16. Threatening, intimidating, coercing or abusing fellow employees, or any attempt to retard the work of fellow employees or otherwise disturb or interfere with them on the Employer's premises.
17. Lying to superiors in connection with their work.
18. Absence from work without receipt of proper notice by the Employer, unless failure to give such notice was due to circumstances beyond the control of the employee. The procedure for reporting absences from work is covered in a separate memorandum.
19. Absence from work where permission to be absent has not been given by the Employer, unless such absence is beyond the control of the employee.
20. Being late for work two (2) or more times in any thirty (30) day period without reasonable excuse.
21. Harboring a disease which may endanger the health of fellow employees.
22. Making disparaging remarks about the Employer or the products sold by the Employer or any words or deeds which would discourage any person from dealing with the Employer.
23. Prowling about the premises of the Employer without justifiable reason.
24. Changing assigned working places without permission.
25. Neglect in the care or use of the Employer's property.
26. Use of habit-forming drugs or narcotics or their introduction or possession on the property of the Employer.
27. Abuse of break periods.
28. Punching another employee's time card, or failure of an employee to properly punch his time card, during work hours.
29. Early punching of an employee's time card, or failure of an employee to properly punch his time card after work hours.
30. Improperly reporting piecework or incentive work, including the performance of any portion of a piecework or incentive job while on downtime or assisting, while on downtime, another employee who is working on a piecework or incentive basis.
31. Misuse or removal from the Employer's premises, without proper autho-

rization, of employee lists, Employer records, blueprints, or confidential information of any kind.

32. Unauthorized distribution of literature, written or printed matter on the Employer's premises, or posting or removing of notices, signs or writing in any form on bulletin boards or other property of the Employer. However, employees may distribute Union literature on Company premises before or after work or during lunch or break periods, provided that the employee distributing the Union literature and the employee receiving the Union literature are both off work or on lunch or break periods at the time of the distribution.

33. Unauthorized operation or use of any machines, tools, equipment or other property of the Employer.

34. Negligence or carelessness resulting in damage or destruction to or loss of the Employer's property.

35. Failure to follow safety rules, or failure to use safety devices or appliances.

36. Unauthorized solicitations or collections for any purpose on the Employer's premises. However, solicitations of Union membership on Company premises are permissible before or after work or during break or lunch periods, provided that the employee doing the soliciting and the employee solicited are both off work or on break or lunch periods at the time of the solicitation.

37. Gambling or participation in games of chance on the Employer's premises.

38. Excessive absenteeism.

39. Tampering with or removing safety devices.

40. Any other act of dishonesty, gross misconduct, or gross neglect not listed above.

(b) Except as provided in paragraph (a), violation of the offenses listed below shall not be cause for immediate discharge, but the offending employee shall be subject to a reprimand for a first offense, layoff up to five (5) working days for the second offense, and discharge for a third offense. For the purpose of this paragraph (b), . . . at the end of each two (2) year period . . . any warning slips issued by the Employer during said two (2) year period shall be disregarded. The employer may impose lesser penalties than those provided for in this paragraph (b) if he wishes. In [the] assessing [of] penalties, the second or third offense does not have to be the same type or kind as the first or second offense. The offenses which are subject to the said sequence of penalties shall include, but are not limited to, the following:

1. Reporting back to work late or stopping work early (lunch hour and rest periods included), or leaving own department before quitting time.

2. Failure or inability or lack of effort to perform work in accordance with recognized standards of performance, as to both quality and quantity.

3. Work of a personal nature, loitering, reading (other than in connection with the employee's job), visiting other departments without authorization, or other time wasting during working hours.
4. Engaging in horseplay, distracting [the] attention of others or creating disturbances, making derogatory statements to or concerning other employees, or unnecessary shouting, catcalls or demonstrations.
5. Smoking in unauthorized areas or during unauthorized times; wasting time or loitering in toilets or smoking rooms or elsewhere during working hours.
6. Creating or contributing to unsanitary or dirty conditions.
7. Absenteeism.
8. Lateness.
9. Loafing.
10. Uncooperative attitude.
11. Acts of disrespect toward customers or visitors on Employer's premises.
12. Garnishment or assignment of wages.
13. Working before a shift starts, after a shift ends, or during lunch or break periods.
14. Any other just cause.

(c) Failure of the Employer to enforce any of the provisions of this Supplemental Agreement in any one or more instances shall not be considered a waiver of any of the provisions of this Supplemental Agreement.

SPECIMEN 3

Agreement between Mount Sinai Hospital, New York, N.Y., and Drug & Hospital Employees, AFL-CIO.

Employees are entitled to retain their jobs on the basis of good behavior, efficiency, and honesty. The Hospital shall have the right to discipline or discharge any employee who fails to meet the foregoing conditions, and particularly, but without limitation, offenses against Hospital discipline as listed in Appendix C, annexed to and made part of this Agreement.

Notwithstanding the provisions of Section C of this Article and Article XXII, a discharge or suspension based upon improper conduct of an employee towards a patient shall not be subject to the grievance and arbitration procedure. Should the Union claim, however, that an employee was discharged or suspended for reasons other than improper conduct of an employee towards patients, such latter issue, as distinguished from the question of improper conduct, may be submitted to the grievance and arbitration procedure.

APPENDIX C

Principal Offenses Against Hospital Discipline

The following list includes the principal offenses against Hospital discipline, as established by the Hospital. Punishment for these offenses shall range from verbal reprimand to dismissal:

1. Falsification of Employment Record or other Hospital records.
2. Failure to ring the time card, ringing another employee's time card, or permitting another employee to ring one's time card.
3. Unauthorized absence from post of duty during regularly scheduled tour of duty.
4. Loafing or sleeping while on duty.
5. Refusal to follow instructions of the duly assigned supervisor; refusal to accept a job assignment; insubordination.
6. Use of vile, intemperate, or abusive language.
7. Immoral or illegal conduct.
8. Use of or unauthorized possession of intoxicating beverages on the Hospital's premises, or reporting to work under the influence of intoxicants.
9. Use of narcotics, except by prescription.
10. Threatening, intimidating, or coercing another employee.
11. Fighting, horseplay, annoying another employee, or other disorderly conduct on the Hospital's premises.
12. Possession of a weapon on the Hospital's premises.
13. Gambling, conducting games of chance, or possession of gambling devices on the Hospital's premises.
14. Creating unsafe or unsanitary conditions, or contributing to such conditions by acts or omission.
15. Smoking in unauthorized areas, or smoking at unauthorized times.
16. Unauthorized possession, use, copying, or reading of Hospital records, or disclosure of information contained in such records to unauthorized persons.
17. Larceny, misappropriation, or unauthorized possession or use of property belonging to the Hospital or to any employee, patient, or visitor.
18. Excessive absence or tardiness.
19. Negligence or deliberate destruction or misuse of Hospital property or property of another employee, patient, or visitor.
20. Any wilful act or conduct detrimental to patient care or Hospital operations.
21. Disregard concerning personal appearance, uniforms, dress, or personal hygiene.
22. Going to or being found in cafeteria, coffee shop, or snack bar at times other than those authorized.

23. Soliciting or accepting tips from patients, visitors, or staff.
24. Failure to render a personal service to any patient if such service is within the normal and usual scope of the employee's duties or is required by reason of an emergency relating to the patient.

SPECIMEN 4

Agreement between Swan Rubber Division (Amerace ESNA Corp.) and the United Rubber Workers Union.

All infractions of Company rules, as shown in the Appendix hereto, [of] which official notice has been taken shall be noted by the Company in writing and shall become a part of the employee's service record, but only after a copy of the charge has been furnished to the employee who is accused. If the employee is later exonerated, such charge shall be stricken from the service record.

APPENDIX

Notification of Conditions Which May Result in Reprimand

1. Working Time—Employees reporting for work shall be at their respective places of work at their scheduled starting time. They shall remain at work until their scheduled stopping time, except for brief necessary or excused absences.
2. Tardiness—Habitual tardiness will render an employee subject to a reprimand.

Notification of Conditions Which May Result in Suspension

1. Multiple Reprimands—Any employee who receives three reprimands may be subject to suspension.
2. Defective Workmanship—Excessive waste of materials or continued defective workmanship.
3. Insubordination.

Notification of Conditions Which May Result in Discharge

1. Multiple Reprimands—For the same offense.
2. Multiple Suspensions—For the same offense.
3. Misrepresentation—Employees misrepresenting material facts in obtaining employment with the Company will be subject to dismissal. . . .

SPECIMEN 5

Agreement involving the United Automobile, Aircraft and Agricultural Implement Workers of America.

Shop Rules and Penalties

Reporting for work or working under the influence of liquor or having intoxicating liquors in possession. First offense—discharge.

Running through plant at any time except in emergencies. This includes entering or leaving the plant. First offense—warning; second offense—warning to three days off; third offense—one week off and sixty days' probation; fourth offense—discharge.

Horseplay. First offense—warning; second offense—one week off and sixty days' probation; third offense—discharge.

Loitering in rest rooms or in any other place where the employee's duties do not call for his presence. First offense—warning; second offense—warning and sixty days' probation; third offense—one week off and sixty days' probation; fourth offense—discharge.

Sleeping on duty. First offense—warning; second offense—discharge.

Failure to perform work as ordered. First offense—warning; second offense—one week off and sixty days' probation; third offense—discharge.

Deliberate misrepresentation or falsification of records. First offense—one week off and sixty days' probation; second offense—discharge.

Conducting gambling devices, games, lotteries, punch boards, or bookmaking. First offense—warning; second offense—six days off; third offense—discharge.

Assault and assault and battery within the meaning of and as defined by the laws of the State of Michigan. First offense—one week off; second offense—discharge.

Stealing. First offense—discharge.

Carrying concealed firearms. First offense—discharge.

Habitual tardiness. First offense—warning; second offense—one week off and sixty days' probation; third offense—discharge.

Hoarding tools, gauges, or materials. First offense—warning; second offense—one week off and sixty days' probation; third offense—discharge.

Quitting work before proper time except when authorized by foreman or rules. First offense—warning; second offense—warning; third offense—one week off and sixty days' probation; fourth offense—discharge.

Tampering with or damaging equipment or gauges so as to produce scrap or hold up work. First offense—Company will report to Federal officials and discharge.

Any action, verbal or physical, on the part of any employee detrimental or disruptive to harmonious relations between employees. First offense—warning; second offense—one week off and sixty days' probation; third offense—discharge.

Conduct unbecoming to an employee and the making of vile, obscene, and provocative remarks. First offense—warning; second offense—three days off; third offense—one week off; fourth offense—discharge.

It will be necessary for every employee of this Company to wear a proper identification badge at all times while on Company property. When a man appears at work without his badge, he will either be given a temporary badge or [be] sent home after his badge, depending upon the circumstances of the case. An employee will be charged 50¢ for each lost badge.

All employees leaving the plant before the end of a shift will [need] a pass from the foreman which is to be presented to the Plant Protection at the point of exit. The penalty for leaving without a pass will be ninety (90) days on probation and one week off during [those] ninety days, the week to be chosen by the Company some time during the probationary period.

It will be a violation of our posted rule on falsification of records for one employee to ring in or ring out another employee's time card.

Any employee leaving the plant or going to the office or other department on personal business must have a written pass from his foreman.

A package pass must be secured from the foreman to remove any property from the premises except lunch boxes and clothing belonging to employees.

If the physical condition of any employee is such that it may impair his own welfare or that of his fellow workers, he will not be permitted to work.

SPECIMEN 6

Agreement involving the United Automobile, Aircraft and Agricultural Implement Workers of America.

Safety Rules

The prevention of accidents in this shop is one of your most important duties to yourself, to your family and to your fellow workers.

Fooling, scuffling or throwing "things" about the shop will not be tolerated.

The use of compressed air for any purposes other than that usually necessary for the performance of the work is strictly forbidden.

Goggles must be worn as instructed.

Loose clothing, rings and neckties are not to be worn around revolving machinery. Keep sleeves rolled up.

Shut down your machine when oiling, greasing, cleaning or repairing it, if necessary, in the interest of safety.

Electricity should not be fooled with. If there are any repairs or adjustments necessary, call for the electrician.

Guards and safety devices are always to be used and kept in place.

Report any dangerous conditions or defective machine to your foreman.

Do not touch a person who is operating a machine. If you wish to tell him something, wait until he has completed the piece or has stopped the machine.

Never leave a board with nails turned up. Turn them down or remove them.

In cases of injury in the shop, no matter how slight, be sure to receive treatment immediately at the First Aid Office.

Do not allow anyone but the First Aid Attendant to remove foreign bodies from your eyes or treat an eye injury. Blindness or serious infection often results from amateur treatment.

When an injury in the plant confines you to your home, notify the Company at once so that you may receive the proper attention.

Appendix B

Specimen Forms
of Special Clauses
on Disciplinary Action
and Discharges

The following specimens of clauses on disciplinary action and discharges have been excerpted verbatim from various contracts. Identification has been supplied where it was available.

SPECIMEN 1

Agreement between Johnson & Johnson and Textile Workers Union, AFL-CIO.

Discharge Subject to Grievance Procedure

The Employer shall have the right to suspend or to discharge employees. The Union shall have the right to take up any suspension or discharge case, except the suspension or discharge of a probationary employee, as a grievance within five (5) working days after such suspension or discharge takes place, and such case shall be subject to review under the grievance and arbitration procedure beginning at Step 3.

159

SPECIMEN 2

**Agreement between Carnegie-Illinois Steel Corp.
and United Steelworkers of America, CIO.**

Suspension Before Discharge—Grievance Procedure— Reinstatement with
Back Pay After Unjustified Discharge

In the exercise of its rights as set forth in Section 10, Management agrees
that an employee shall not be peremptorily discharged from and after the
date hereof, but that in all instances in which Management may conclude
that an employee's conduct may justify suspension or discharge, he shall
be first suspended. Such initial suspension shall be for not more than five
(5) calendar days. During this period of initial suspension the employee
may, if he believes that he has been unjustly dealt with, request a hearing
and a statement of the offense before his department head with or without
an assistant grievance committeeman or grievance committeeman present
as he may choose, or the General Superintendent, or the Manager of the
Plant with or without the member or members of the grievance committee
present, as he similarly may choose. At such hearing the facts concerning
the case shall be made available to both parties. After such hearing or if no
such hearing is requested Management may conclude whether the suspension shall be converted into a discharge or, dependent upon the facts of the
case, that such suspension should be extended or revoked. If the suspension
is revoked the employee shall be returned to employment and receive full
compensation at his regular rate of pay for the time lost, but in the event a
disposition shall result in either the affirmation or extension of the suspension
or discharge of the employee, the employee may within five (5) calendar
days after such disposition allege a grievance which shall be handled in
accordance with the procedure of Section 9—Adjustment of Grievances.
Final decision on all suspension or discharge cases shall be made by the
Company within five (5) calendar days from the date of filing of the grievance, if any. Should it be determined by the Company or in arbitration that
the employee has been discharged or suspended unjustly, the Company shall
reinstate the employee and pay full compensation at the employee's regular
rate of pay for the time lost.

SPECIMEN 3

**Agreement between Otis Elevator Co. and Metropolitan Federation
of Architects, Engineers, Chemists & Technicians, UOPWA, CIO.**

Discharge for Unsatisfactory Work—Thirty-Day Warning

No employee covered by this Agreement shall be discharged for unsatisfactory work without first having received written warning as to his de-

ficiency and a reasonable opportunity to improve his work, generally not less than thirty (30) working days. No warning need be given an employee before discharging him for any other proper cause.

SPECIMEN 4

Agreement between United States Steel Corporation and United Steelworkers, AFL-CIO.

Suspension Before Discharge; Hearing and Presentation of Grievance; Reinstatement with Full Pay

An employee shall not be peremptorily discharged. In all cases in which Management may conclude that an employee's conduct may justify suspension or discharge, he shall be suspended initially for not more than 5 calendar days, and given written notice of such action. . . . If such initial suspension is for 5 calendar days and if the employee affected believes that he has been unjustly dealt with, he may request and shall be granted, during this period, a hearing and a statement of the offense before a representative (status of department head or higher) designated by the General Superintendent of the plant with or without an assistant grievance committeeman or grievance committeeman present as the employee may choose. . . . In the event the suspension is affirmed, modified, extended, or converted into a discharge, the employee may, within 5 calendar days after notice of such action, file a grievance in the third step of the grievance procedure. . . . Should any initial suspension, or affirmation, modification, or extension thereof, or discharge be revoked by the Company, the Company shall reinstate and compensate the employee affected on the basis of an equitable lump sum payment mutually agreed to by the parties or, in the absence of agreement, make him whole in the manner set forth in Section 8-D below.

SPECIMEN 5

Agreement involving the United Automobile, Aircraft and Agricultural Implement Workers of America, CIO.

(a) All disciplinary action shall be for cause. The Company agrees that it will notify the Union in writing of the reason for any disciplinary layoff or discharge and will also provide an opportunity for any employee laid off or discharged to contact his steward at a place in the plant designated by the Company, as soon as the employee has left his department.

(b) Any grievance involving a disciplinary layoff (but not a discharge) must be filed in writing on the standard grievance form with the Plant Superintendent within two working days of the notification of, or the taking of, the disciplinary layoff action, and shall be disposed of in accordance with the grievance procedure. . . .

(c)   In the event of a contemplated discharge the Company may lay off the employee, but as soon as discharge is proposed the Company shall notify him and the Chairman of the Plant Committee. Unless objection is filed by the employee or the Plant Committee with the Industrial Relations Department prior to the close of the second succeeding working day following such notification, the employee may be discharged at once or otherwise disciplined. Should objection be made, it shall be filed in writing on the standard grievance form and disposed of as a grievance under the grievance procedure. . . .

(d)   In the event that it shall be determined that any disciplinary layoff or discharge of any employee was unwarranted, the employee shall be reinstated without loss of seniority and given back pay for the time lost thereby in an amount equal to what he would have earned for the hours lost on the basis of his average earnings for the pay period immediately preceding the date of his layoff or discharge.

(e)   In the event that [a] disciplinary layoff is made on a Sunday or a holiday forming the basis of a grievance by the Union and requiring the calling to the plant of a steward, the time spent in handling the grievance by the steward on such Sunday or holiday shall be paid for aside from the time allowed and paid for under Section 2, Article II, hereof.

SPECIMEN 6

Agreement involving International Association of Machinists, AFL.

After the 45-day probationary period, the Employer reserves to itself the unrestricted right to discharge an employee for just cause. It agrees, however, that except for theft, insubordination, habitual drunkenness, deliberate falsification of record of work performed, or willful injury to the Employer's property or to persons on its premises, it will not discharge an employee as herein defined for inefficiency or acts of omission or violations of the published Shop Rules unless such employee and the Shop Committee shall have been warned in writing that a repetition thereof or further or other violations of his duties as an employee will result in his discharge.

In the event an employee should be unjustly laid off or discharged, such employee shall be restored to service with rights unimpaired and paid for all time lost. Such employee shall be required to submit a written grievance within forty-eight (48) hours to [the] Shop Steward and such grievance to be settled as expeditiously as possible.

The term "discharge" does not include layoffs for the purpose of reducing the Employer's force of workmen.

SPECIMEN 7

Agreement involving International Association of Machinists, AFL.

In the event that an employee is disciplined or discharged, he shall be given a plain and logical reason in writing for such action. If the employee is dissatisfied he must file a written complaint with the Company within twenty-four (24) hours from his dismissal. The Company and the Union shall jointly investigate the reasons for the dismissal and shall agree or disagree with the action by the Company within seventy-two (72) hours from the time of his dismissal. In the case of a disagreement within said time, the said parties shall agree upon a third disinterested person to investigate the dismissal, and the decision of any two shall be final and binding upon the employee and the parties hereto. The final decision must be rendered not later than one (1) week after the time of dismissal, and if the decision be that the dismissal was not justified, the employee shall be reinstated and reimbursed for loss of wages suffered by him. In no event shall any such employee be entitled to recover wages for more than three (3) weeks of five (5) days each, pending the final disposition of such investigation and complaint.

SPECIMEN 8

Agreement between Overhead Door Corp. and United Brotherhood of Carpenters & Joiners, AFL-CIO.

Removal of Employee from Job for Unsatisfactory Production

When an employee does not meet the production quantity and quality standard as established for the particular job on which he is working, his foreman will make an effort to determine the reasons therefor and discuss the matter with the employee. A record shall be made of such effort and discussion which record shall be signed by the foreman and by the employee. If, as a result of and after such discussion, [the] standard is not then reached and there is a continued failure or refusal of the employee to meet the production standard, the same shall be considered due cause for discipline, and the Employer shall have the right to determine who should be disciplined in a group operation for failure of the group to meet production standards. If demotion or removal from the job is determined upon, the Employer may place the employee affected on any job which may be available within the capacities of the employee, and if there be no such available job then the employee shall be laid off to await an opening on an available job.

SPECIMEN 9

**Agreement between Carborundum Company
and United Electrical Radio & Machine Workers.**

The Company agrees that a member of the Union shall not be per-emptorily discharged but that in all instances in which the Company may conclude that an employee's conduct may justify discharge, he shall first be suspended. This initial suspension shall not be for more than three (3) working days.

Upon being notified of the suspension it shall be the duty of the employee to leave his Department and go to the Personnel Office. The Chief Steward shall be notified immediately and be given the opportunity to review the case with the employee. At the conclusion of this meeting, the employee shall leave the plant, if it is impossible to schedule a meeting as outlined in Section 21 below.

During a period of initial suspension, the Union or the employee may, if it is believed that he has been unjustly dealt with, request a hearing before his foreman, the Personnel and/or the Plant Manager or his authorized representative, with the Chief Steward or any other Union representative present if the employee so desires. . . . If the suspension is revoked, the employee shall be returned to employment and will receive full compensation at his regular rate of pay for time lost; if the suspension is converted into discharge or disciplinary layoff the Union or the employee may, within five (5) working days after such disposition, file a protest with the Personnel Manager. In that event the matter will be disposed of promptly in the Grievance Procedure as outlined in Article VII of this Agreement and will be heard in the first instance in Step C, and where Step D is used special efforts will be made to expedite the case. If under that procedure it is agreed or decided that an injustice has been done, the action will be modified as may be necessary to correct the injustice, including where appropriate reinstatement and payment for time unjustly lost from work.

SPECIMEN 10

**Agreement between Doughnut Corp. of America
and United Office and Professional Workers of America, CIO.**

When an employee shall be dismissed or shall resign, the Employer shall, upon request of the employee, issue a true statement of his or her character and service; such statement shall not be used nor shall it be admissible at any hearing contesting such dismissal or in any litigation whatsoever.

SPECIMEN 11

Agreement between Gardner-Denver Company and United Steelworkers of America.

Section 1. The Company retains the right to establish and enforce shop rules and regulations. It is understood that such rules and regulations will not impair or abridge the provisions of this Agreement. Violation of such rules and regulations may be cause for suspension or discharge.

Section 2. Rules and regulations governing employees covered by this Agreement shall be discussed with the Union prior to their effectiveness. Any disciplinary action taken by the Company pursuant to such rules and regulations may be made the subject of a grievance.

SPECIMEN 12

Agreement between the Great Western Sugar Company and Teamsters, Warehousemen and Sugar Workers.

Good cause for discipline or discharge of employees shall be in the Company's discretion. The Company shall furnish each discharged employee a copy of the Time Order indicating thereon the reason for his discharge. Any employee who believes that he has been unjustly disciplined or discharged may avail himself of the grievance procedure provided in this Article. Any employee who is found to have been unjustly disciplined or discharged shall be returned to his former status of employment and seniority.

SPECIMEN 13

Agreement involving the United Automobile, Aircraft and Agricultural Implement Workers, CIO.

The Company agrees to post in each department a copy of general shop rules and regulations of the Company having plantwide effect, but these rules and regulations shall not be so devised as to abridge the rights of employees guaranteed by this Agreement. Any additions to or changes in such rules and regulations may be made either by adding to or [by] amending the regularly posted rules above mentioned or by posting special bulletins on Company bulletin boards. Such additions or changes to the rules and regulations shall be effective 48 hours after such addition, amendment or posting. Violation by any employee of shop rules or of any provisions of this Agreement shall be cause for discipline.

SPECIMEN 14

Agreement involving the United Automobile, Aircraft and Agricultural Implement Workers, CIO.

It is mutually recognized that the maintenance of discipline is a function of Management. The disciplinary action should be for just cause. Cause for such action shall include the following: Repeated inadequate performance of work, breakage of equipment due to carelessness, reporting for work under the influence of liquor, repeated insubordination, conviction of a felony or any other act or action contrary to the benefit of the parties. Disciplinary action shall take the form of an immediate layoff not to exceed one calendar week, during which time the Company and the Bargaining Committee shall meet and make final disposition of the case. Any such decision reached shall be final.

SPECIMEN 15

Agreement involving the United Automobile, Aircraft and Agricultural Implement Workers, CIO.

The Company will notify the chief steward of any disciplinary action that has been taken against any employee. Copies of all warnings presented to employees shall also be given to the chief steward. Any employee who claims he has been discharged without just cause may file a signed complaint with his foreman within 24 hours of his discharge and a copy with a member of the Bargaining Committee, and if he does so, the Bargaining Committee and a representative of Management with the employee's foreman will meet at once in respect to the claim. If the employee is upheld, the Company will reimburse him for his lost time. Before leaving the plant a discharged employee shall be entitled to interview his committeeman or his chief steward, if his committeeman or his chief steward is in the plant at the time, such interview to take place in the watchman's office.

References

Abbreviations used in the citations that follow

ALAA	*American Labor Arbitration Awards*
A.L.R.2d	*American Law Reports Annotated,* Second Series (1948-1965)
Ann.Cas.	*American & English Annotated Cases*
ARB	*Labor Arbitration Awards* (CCH)
Arb. J.	*Arbitration Journal*
BNA	Bureau of National Affairs
CCH	Commerce Clearing House
Colo.	*Colorado Reports*
ENF	*Enforcing*
Harv. L. Rev.	*Harvard Law Review*
LA	*Labor Arbitration Reports* (BNA)
LRA	Labor Relations Act
LRRM	*Labor Relations Reference Manual* (BNA; 1935 to date)
LRX	*Labor Relations Expediter* (BNA)
Mich. L. Rev.	*Michigan Law Review*
N.E.	*North Eastern Reporter*
O.Jur.2d	*Ohio Jurist,* Second Series
O.S.	Ohio State Reports

Chapter 1
1. See 46 LRRM 2416.
2. *Collective Bargaining Negotiations and Contracts, Annual Labor Contracts Survey* (BNA 1969).
3. *Loc. cit.*
4. See 42 LRRM 2034.

167

5. See 54 LRRM 1327.
6. See 45 LA 530.
7. See 25 LA 295.
8. See 25 LA 300-301.
9. See Shulman, "Reason, Contract and Law in Labor Relations," 68 *Harv. L. Rev.* 999 (1955).
10. See 32 LA 753.
11. See 24 LA 453.
12. See 22 LA 761.
13. See 13 LA 747.
14. See 43 LA 689.
15. See 51 LRRM 2752 and 52 LRRM 2764.
16. See 8 LRRM 1038.
17. See 41 LA 76.
18. See 41 LA 211.
19. See 44 LA 733.
20. For additional cases dealing with absenteeism, see Chapter 4.
21. See 42 LA 769.
22. See 28 LA 829.
23. See 44 LA 224.
24. See 43 LA 337.
25. See 32 LA 865.
26. See 41 LA 1039. For additional cases relating to the establishment of rules by an employer, see 43 LA 465, 31 LA 836 and 865, 11 LA 689, 7 LA 150, and 5 LA 60.
27. See 42 LA 1162. For additional cases involving production standards, see 41 LA 953, 32 LA 317, 42 LA 298 and 1127, 43 LA 1208, 35 LA 575, and 33 LA 913.
28. See 28 LRRM 1579.
29. See 10 LRRM 483.
30. See 33 LRRM 2417.
31. See 19 LRRM 2009.
32. For cases involving the various points enumerated here, see 22 LRRM 2089, 29 LRRM 2420, 51 LRRM 1193, 25 LRRM 2340, 24 LRRM 1216, 31 LRRM 2242, 56 LRRM 2034, 14 LRRM 271, 38 LRRM 2276, 18 LRRM 1440, 7 LRRM 69 and 120, 11 LRRM 74, 17 LRRM 441, 12 LRRM 94 and 108, 10 LRRM 61, 9 LRRM 286, and 16 LRRM 202.
33. See 28 LRRM 2427 and 1298.
34. See 29 LRRM 2379.
35. See 29 LRRM 1482.
36. See 29 LRRM 2302.
37. See 29 LRRM 2290.
38. See 29 LRRM 1105.
39. See 29 LRRM 2331.
40. See, for example, 31 LRRM 2082.

Chapter 2
1. See 46 LRRM 2416.
2. *Ibid.*
3. See 29 LA 458 and 22 LA 756.
4. See 24 LA 1 and 453 and 29 LA 567.
5. See 45 LA 1124; see also 39 LA 931.
6. See 2 LA 558.
7. See 10 LA 207.
8. See 7 LA 764.
9. See 29 LA 451.
10. See 47 LA 1104.
11. See 45 LA 515 and 42 LA 555.
12. For examples of this, see 24 LA 630 and 22 LA 756.
13. See 36 LA 552.
14. See 38 LA 778.
15. See 13 LA 747.
16. See Chapter 1 for a discussion on this subject.
17. See 24 LA 680.
18. See 39 LA 352, 29 LA 272, and 24 LA 804.
19. See 1 LA 254.
20. United Steelworkers of America, Arbitration Bulletin No. 17, 1970.
21. See 7 LA 147.
22. See 2 LA 194.
23. See 42 LA 803.
24. See 43 LA 400.
25. See *Pawnee* v. *Farmers Elevator and Supply Co.*, 76 Colo. 1 and 227, P2d 836.
26. See 39 LA 470; see also 45 LA 490 and 40 LA 598.
27. See 42 LA 583.
28. See 29 LA 291, 20 LA 451, and 19 LA 417.
29. See 33 LA 735.
30. New York: New York University, Practising Law Institute, 1959, II, 492.
31. See 23 A.L.R.2d 1308.
32. Fleming, "The Polygraph and the Arbitration Process," 60 *Mich. L. Rev.* (1961), p. 12; reprinted as Reprint Series No. 111 (Urbana: University of Illinois, Institute of Labor and Industrial Relations, 1969).
33. See 38 LA 778.
34. See 45 LA 1155.
35. See 31 LA 515.
36. See 43 LA 450.
37. Burkey, "Lie Detectors in Labor Relations," 19 *Arb. J.* 193 (1964).
38. See 32 LA 44.
39. See 39 LA 332.
40. See 39 LA 470.
41. See 46 LA 95.

Chapter 3

1. See the section "Some Arbitral Views on Just Cause."
2. American Arbitration Association, *Arb. J.* (Nov. 1969).
3. See "Substantive Aspects of Labor-Management Arbitration," 28 LA 943.
4. See 53 LA 410.
5. See 69-1 ARB 8334.
6. See 28 LA 330.
7. See 23 LA 252.
8. See 25 LA 736.
9. See 17 LA 580.
10. See 29 LA 167.
11. See 26 LA 245.
12. See 12 LA 266, 17 LA 328, and 18 LA 457.
13. See 18 LA 368 and 24 LA 470.
14. See 11 LA 598.
15. See 53 LA 1100.
16. See 53 LA 400; see also 53 LA 521.
17. See 18 LA 576.
18. See 27 LA 11, 11 LA 354, 22 LA 238, 16 LA 290, and 3 LA 461.
19. See, for example, 24 LA 314, 11 LA 965, 8 LA 259, and 5 LA 22.
20. See 53 LA 1103.
21. See 53 LA 689.
22. See 41 LA 804.
23. See 62 LRRM 1306 and 68 LRRM 1243.
24. See 26 LRRM 1005.
25. See 9 LRRM 21.
26. See 22 LRRM 1178.
27. See 41 LA 1184; see also 29 LA 129.
28. See 42 LA 849.
29. See 29 LA 700.
30. See 22 LA 238.
31. See 44 LA 604.
32. See 53 LA 125.
33. See 47 LA 994.
34. *Ibid.*
35. See 43 LA 634.
36. *Ibid.*
37. See 30 LA 199.
38. See 28 LA 875.
39. See 43 LA 31.
40. See 12 LA 344.
41. See 32 LA 586.
42. See 16 LA 616.
43. See 12 LA 129.
44. See 16 LA 616.

45. See 35 LA 95.
46. See 35 LA 293.
47. *Management Rights and the Arbitration Process* (BNA, 1956), p. 81.
48. See 45 LA 1128, 24 LA 132, and 42 LA 947.
49. 45 LA 398.
50. See 37 LA 1003.
51. See 43 LA 511.
52. See 44 LA 920.
53. See 45 LA 498, 29 LA 442, 26 LA 570, and 22 LA 851.
54. See 46 LA 124; see also 29 LA 443.
55. See 53 LA 85.
56. See 36 LA 1386.
57. See 37 LA 847.

Chapter 4
1. See 31 LA 867.
2. See 39 LA 286.
3. See LRX sec. 143 (1969).
4. See 23 LA 663, 18 LA 869, 15 LA 593, and LRX sec. 159 (1969).
5. See 12 LA 770 and 11 LA 947.
6. See 11 LA 419.
7. See 39 LA 187.
8. See 53 LA 594.
9. See 66-1 ARB 8245.
10. See 49 LA 1257.
11. See 41 LA 1257.
12. See 62-3 ARB 9070.
13. See 36 LA 1307.
14. See 64 ARB 8015.
15. *Ibid.*
16. See 39 LA 187.
17. See 66-3 ARB 8747.
18. See 36 LA 1392.
19. See 45 LA 108.
20. See 52 LA 488.
21. See 52 LA 861.
22. See 52 LA 677.
23. See 21 LA 105.
24. See 12 LA 641.
25. See 21 LA 314.
26. See 43 LA 400.
27. See 40 LA 1084.
28. See 45 LA 53.
29. William O. Douglas, *An Almanac of Liberty* (Doubleday, Garden City, N.Y., 1954), pp. 178 and 372.

30. See 28 LA 829, 27 LA 128, and 21 LA 80.
31. See 25 LA 709, 20 LA 50, 28 LA 226, and 19 LA 733.
32. See 32 LA 293.
33. See 41 LA 888.
34. See 31 LA 832.
35. See 25 LA 568.
36. See 43 LA 838.
37. See 43 LA 753; see also 41 LA 1179 and 31 LA 68.
38. See 44 LA 1043.
39. See 29 LA 182, 21 LA 560, and 17 LA 230.
40. See 3 ALAA 68, S408; see also 19 LA 854 and 203, 14 LA 381, and 12 LA 207.
41. See 31 LA 1018.
42. See 15 LA 318.
43. See 31 LA 599.
44. See 32 LA 153.
45. This principle may also apply to off-duty behavior in circumstances such as those explored in Chapter 5. With regard to off-premises fights, see the section "Feuding" in that chapter.
46. See 35 LA 293.
47. See 27 LA 279 and 15 LA 372.
48. See 21 LA 32 and 41 LA 838.
49. See 12 LA 682.
50. See 5 O.Jur.2d 107; see also 70 O.Sup. 179, 71 N.E. 633 and 665, LRA 860, and 1 Ann.Cas. 896.
51. See 41 LA 442; see also 44 LA 499.
52. See 44 LA 493.
53. See 41 LA 575.
54. See 33 LA 295.
55. See 44 LA 254; see also 44 LA 507.
56. See 43 LA 864.
57. See 45 LA 437.
58. See 23 LA 284.
59. See 22 LA 1210.
60. See 12 LA 699 and 18 LA 938.
61. See 28 LA 97.
62. See 16 LA 727.
63. See 17 LA 150.
64. See 16 LA 727.
65. See 45 LA 1007.
66. See 32 LA 26.
67. See 33 LA 174.
68. See 44 LA 343.
69. See 44 LA 921.
70. See 44 LA 730.
71. *Ibid.*

72. Researched in Bureau of National Affairs, Inc., Washington, D.C., Labor Arbitration Reports, Volumes 11–54, 1949 to 1971.
73. See also "Discipline and Discharge in the Unionized Firm," by Orme W. Phelps, University of California Press, Berkeley and Los Angeles, 1959.
74. See 42 LA 298.
75. See 42 LA 710.
76. See 42 LA 307.
77. See 42 LA 412.
78. See 41 LA 974.
79. See the section on statutory limitations in Chapter 1.
80. See 5 LRRM 806, 16 LRRM 501, 23 LRRM 1380, and 35 LRRM 1265.
81. See, for example, 41 LA 868.
82. See 44 LA 565.
83. See 44 LA 1139.
84. See 24 LA 163, 1 LA 468, and 11 LA 1158.
85. See 31 LA 567.
86. See 20 LA 480.
87. See 22 LA 138.
88. See 41 LA 283.
89. See 21 LA 617.
90. See 41 LA 796.
91. See 43 LA 640.
92. See 23 LA 269.
93. See 43 LA 678.
94. See 15 LA 903, 20 LA 266, and 12 LA 9.
95. See 28 LA 333 and 26 LA 245.
96. See 22 LA 1, 24 LA 229, and 15 LA 42.
97. See 28 LA 891.
98. See 25 LA 50.
99. See 23 LA 214.
100. See 25 LA 50. For other cases, see 50 LA 597, 645, 965, and 1177; 46 LA 302; 45 LA 500; and 42 LA 559.
101. Bendix Aviation Corp., Eclipse-Pioneer Div., Teterboro, New Jersey, and Aircraft Workers Union of New Jersey, Inc.
102. Maidenform, Inc., Bayonne, New Jersey, and International Ladies Garment Workers Union.
103. Labor agreement between Allegron Instrument Co. Inc. and the United Automobile, Aircraft and Agricultural Implement Workers of America—CIO.
104. Labor agreement between Rex Limited, Inc. and the United Automobile, Aircraft and Agricultural Implement Workers of America—CIO.
105. See 44 LA 847.

106. See 43 LA 849.
107. See 38 LA 1109.
108. See 48 LA 189.
109. See 35 LA 103.
110. See 41 LA 591.
111. See 50 LA 571.
112. See 30 LA 213.
113. See 8 LA 837.
114. See 8 LA 897.
115. See 3 LA 786.
116. See 4 LA 430.
117. See 24 LA 48.
118. See 21 LA 457.
119. *Ibid.*
120. See 46 LA 1161; see also 5 LA 3, 6 LA 913, 9 LA 775, and 30 LA 830 for other cases where reinstatement was ordered despite evidence of minor negligence.
121. See 19 LA 380.
122. See 27 LA 512.
123. See 22 LA 498.
124. See 20 LA 50, 21 LA 676, and 26 LA 472.
125. See 27 LA 768.
126. See 53 LA 1214.
127. See 25 LA 906; see also the section "The Burden of Proof" in Chapter 1.
128. See 45 LA 968.
129. See 45 LA 1050.

Chapter 5
 1. See 39 LA 404.
 2. See 28 LA 434.
 3. See 29 LA 451.
 4. See 27 LA 557.
 5. See 28 LA 434.
 6. See 26 LA 480.
 7. See 24 LA 603.
 8. See 20 LA 175.
 9. See 44 LA 428.
10. See 34 LA 636.
11. See 44 LA 552.
12. See 34 LA 636, 27 LA 540, and 26 LA 401.
13. See 39 LA 404.
14. See 34 LA 458.
15. See 38 LA 891.
16. See 43 LA 242.

17. See 64-2 ARB 8748.
18. See 43 LA 900.
19. See 45 LA 283.
20. See 43 LA 242.
21. See 41 LA 460.
22. See 43 LA 977.
23. See 35 LA 227.
24. See Opinion A-132, Ford Motor Company. Ford and UAW (labor arbitration reports of both parties to this agreement).
25. See 7 LA 780 and 3 LA 486.
26. See 31 LA 675, 7 LA 669, 9 LA 592, and 6 LA 363.
27. See 28 LA 312.
28. See 55 LA 133; see also 30 LA 690.
29. See 42 LA 504.
30. See 44 LA 644; see also 42 LA 1013.
31. See 42 LA 446.
32. See 33 LA 902.
33. See 31 LA 547.
34. See 31 LRRM 2432. For the extension of this rule, see 33 LRRM 1114.
35. See 42 LA 626; see also 45 LA 522.
36. See 35 LA 757.
37. See 41 LA 52.
38. See 45 LA 826.
39. See LRX sec. 508 (1967).
40. See 27 LA 321, 28 LA 121, and 24 LA 761.
41. See 25 LA 663 and 774, 14 LA 986, and 24 LA 421. For further discussion of this subject, see the section "Union Activities."
42. See 18 LA 919, 13 LA 294, and 6 LA 617.
43. See 17 LA 227 and 7 LA 583.
44. See 24 LA 95.
45. See 29 LA 23.
46. See 38 LA 1185.
47. See 43 LA 450.
48. See 42 LA 923.
49. See 4 LRRM 515.
50. See 45 LA 366.
51. See 45 LA 490.
52. See 34 LA 383.
53. See 16 LA 307; see also 39 LA 238 and 30 LA 143.
54. See 4 LA 744; 21 LA 239, 421, and 843; 16 LA 99; 9 LA 447; 42 LA 131, 142, 328, and 923; 13 LA 304; and 30 LA 181 and 250.
55. See 28 LA 369; see also 35 LA 699, 20 LA 875, 33 LA 488, and 6 LA 414.
56. See 28 LA 782; 16 LA 99; 29 LA 622; 43 LA 608; 8 LA 758; 30 LA 109, 250, and 562; 34 LA 325 and 607; 33 LA 594; 13 LA 143 and

295; 6 LA 617; 14 LA 475; and 7 LA 648. For a contrary view, see 33 LA 807.

57. See 3 LA 779; see also 6 LA 988, 9 LA 447, and 19 LA 43.

58. See 9 LA 861. For a decision that this principle does not apply to actions falling primarily within the union's domain, see 10 LA 213.

59. See 20 LA 749; see also 2 LA 295.

60. See 42 LA 70. A similar case appears in 30 LA 358.

61. See 10 LA 965.

62. See 34 LA 262; see also 34 LA 332 and 23 LA 311 and 785.

63. See 33 LA 112; see also 9 LA 265.

64. See 10 LA 265. For a contrary opinion, see 17 LA 199.

65. See 8 LA 765. For other cases of discipline imposed on union representatives in their employee role, see 28 LA 543, 15 LA 842, 1 LA 447, 9 LA 765, 43 LA 46, and 33 LA 701.

66. See 34 LA 464; see also 10 LA 372 for a similar case and 33 LA 146 for a contrary decision.

67. See 9 LA 564; see also 25 LRRM 1381.

68. See 64-1 ARB 8376.

69. See 32 LA 719.

70. See 37 LA 1076.

71. See 10 LA 75.

72. See 33 LA 879.

73. See 30 LA 41.

74. See 33 LA 174.

75. See 8 LA 340.

76. See 21 LA 10. For similar cases, see 31 LA 144 and 14 LA 925.

77. See 10 LA 355; see also 9 LA 861.

78. See 33 LA 103.

Chapter 6

1. See *Radio Officers Union* v. *National Labor Relations Board* and *National Labor Relations Board* v. *Teamsters* (*Gaynor News Co.*), 33 LRRM 2417 and 2426 (1954).

2. See 24 LRRM 1463, ENF (1951), and 27 LRRM 2484.

3. See 31 LRRM 2065.

4. See 57 LRRM 1009.

5. See 60 LRRM 2131 and 58 LRRM 2623.

6. See 61 LRRM 1159, ENF (1968), and 69 LRRM 2656.

7. See 28 LRRM 1327 and 30 LRRM 1371.

8. See 67 LRRM 2410.

9. See 46 LRRM 1428.

10. See 34 LRRM 1646.

11. See 38 LRRM 1205.

12. See 68 LRRM 1301.

13. See 50 LA 186.

14. See 43 LA 1073.
15. *Ibid.*
16. See 43 LA 973.
17. See 39 LA 167.
18. See 34 LRRM 1431.
19. See 57 LRRM 1242.
20. See 65 LRRM 2449.
21. See 67 LRRM 2673.
22. See 64 LRRM 2495.
23. See 40 LA 619.
24. See 37 LRRM 2673 and 38 LRRM 2717.

Index